AFTER NORMAL

One Teen's Journey Following
Her Brother's Death

Diane Aggen

Healthy Life Press

After Normal, by Diane Aggen

Published by Healthy Life Press
Website: www.healthylifepress.com
E-mail: healthylifepress@aol.com

Most Healthy Life Press products are available through quality book-stores everywhere, including major online book retailers. Copies of this book and a downloadable e-book version (or both versions packaged together at a discount) are available directly from the publisher. E-mail: healthylifepress@aol.com for information. To arrange quantity discounts or learn of other special offers, e-mail: healthylifepress@aol.com or visit our website: www.healthylifepress.com.

Undesignated biblical references are from the Holy Bible, King James Version.

Cover & Internal Design, Healthy Life Press

Library of Congress Cataloging-in-Publication Data
2008938777

Upton, Diane Aggen (1964-). After Normal

ISBN 978-0-9821466-0-6

1. Death, Grief, Bereavement;
2. Death of a Sibling

First edition, 2008. Printed in the United States of America.

DEDICATION

For David

FOREWORD

Thirty years ago, Diane's life and mine became inter-
twined forever as a result of events that neither of
us would have chosen, but which, even now,
remain fresh in both our minds. Her memoirs in the following pages cover almost exactly the period during
which I ("Pastor B" in this book) served the only church
in that little town in Michigan's Upper Peninsula.

At 28, I was not prepared for any of the tragedies she
describes; perhaps not even for the "normal" duties of
pastoring. From the very first night in that town, when
there was an accident involving two cousins, at least one
of whom appears in Diane's story, through the death of
Diane's brother, to the death of my own son, to the fire
that took six children and their mother ... that whole
time still seems to me like one really long, really bad
dream, interrupted periodically by some memorable
times of friendship and even occasional frivolity.

As her title suggests, "After Normal" can be a long, long
period of adjusting to a new normal, when we would
give our very lives to have things back to the way they
were before, and getting on with our lives seems somehow disloyal to the one who has left us.

I sat with Diane's mother on the grassy bank overlook-
ing the small pond in which David had drowned, and
held her hand as the diver searched the frigid water until
the boy's body was found, dragged out, and immediately transported toward the nearest hospital.

I remember how angry she was for being kept from
seeing his body before they left, and I learned just a little that day about what to say (or what not to say) when
you don't know what to say.

Diane and I first met the day David drowned, and reading in these pages about my own ineptitude at offering

any real solace to her and her sisters during that encounter has been a good reminder of how difficult it really is to come alongside someone when they just need someone to be there and care and help them carry their pain.

Through the years I've read or reviewed scores of books on grief and loss, and even written some, myself. But I don't know of any that describe what can be a very lonely and confusing journey from the perspective of a teen – without embellishment, pious platitudes, easy answers, or perhaps many answers at all.

The latter is fine with me, for as in the case of the biblical character Job, it's the questions that matter, because for each of us, those questions are unique, and we wouldn't bother to ask the ones related to God and faith unless our faith is, deep down, real and alive.

If you are a teen struggling with loss and wondering if anyone has ever felt the way you do, I urge you to read this book. If you're a parent, minister, or counselor trying to understand a teen's struggle with loss, I urge you to read this book – at least twice.

Diane has put her heart on these pages. For that I thank her. You will, too.

"Pastor B."

PREFACE

For years, I suffered my brother's death in silence. I seldom shared my true feelings with anyone and desperately clung to the pain. In doing so, I believed that I was being loyal to David and his memory. If I let go of the pain, I feared, David's memory would be erased.

I also believed that nobody would understand how I felt losing my brother. I watched others in our small town experience loss, but they seemed to gallantly carry on. I was a mess inside but didn't want anyone else to know it. Perhaps, I had thought, the lingering pain would be seen as a sign of weakness.

As I aged, I longed to write about this loss. I had learned that surviving it had made me strong, not weak. I also began to notice others talking about their losses. I vividly remember listening to a celebrity during an interview. She had lost her brother and was recalling her emotions shortly after his death. I was shocked. Everything she described, I had also experienced. She was an adult and I had only been fourteen. Yet, the emotions of anger, pain and disbelief were the same. That was an eye opening moment for me. I had a true epiphany. I knew that I had to tell my story not because it was unusual, but because it was so common.

At some point in our lives, we will lose a loved one. If that loss occurs during the teenage years, it can be especially devastating. We spend those years trying to define ourselves. Who are we? Where do we fit in? Who loves us? Who will we be? The death of someone close to us can send us reeling and those questions become even more difficult to answer.

If you are a teen and you've experienced such a loss, know that you are not alone. There are others who are walking the same path and even others who have walked it before you. I know I did.

If I could, please allow me to give you one piece of advice. Find something to cling to in your darkest hours. Find one thing to care about to see you through the pain. For me, it was basketball. I didn't realize until years later just how much being on that team and playing that sport sustained me. I even think it saved me.

So, find something to sustain and save you. It could be a sport, of course, but it could also be chess club, band, or volunteering. Anything. Anything where you are counted on to show up and participate. You need a reason to get up in the morning. You need a reason to care again as you make this journey.

Here is my journey. This is the way I remember it, although others may remember it differently. Grief can be blinding. Certainly, the exact conversations can't be recounted, but the gist of them remains true. In some instances, I have used initials to protect identities.

After much consideration, I have labeled my chapters according to the season. David died in the spring, so that is the first season. Along with the fall season, I included the school grade I was starting. After the first year passed, I labeled the seasons Second Spring, Third Spring, etc. I do not, in any way, mean to imply that this is a timeline for grief. It is not. It is just a way for you, the reader, to know where I was at that point in time.

Also, please consider my not being able to see color as a metaphor of how I felt inside. It is one thing to see the colors that surround us and quite another to recognize and appreciate them. After losing David, I had to slowly awaken to them and learn to appreciate them anew.

Again, this is the story of my journey. But, if you are a teenager grieving the loss of a loved one, I wrote it for you.

1

End of Eighth Grade
Spring
Day One

*B*reathe. *Please just breathe*, I begged myself as I knelt in the backyard, doubled over and gasping for air, my eyes squeezed shut.

I wanted the ground to open and swallow me whole. I wanted to float towards the sun and never stop. I wanted to go to sleep and never wake. I wanted to wake and have this be a horrible, horrible nightmare. I wanted to start running and never, ever stop. I could just keep running. First, though, I needed to catch my breath.

Inhale. Exhale. Inhale. Exhale. Breathe. That's all. Just breathe. I opened my eyes but quickly shut them again. The grass was too green.

Inhale. Exhale. Each inhale filled my lungs, my heart, my very soul with sorrow. Each exhale left only emptiness.

I could smell the grass just inches from my face. After long, northern Michigan winters, spring was always so welcomed. The blooming trees, blossoming flowers and the greening of the grass assured us that we had survived another winter and, as a reward, we could enjoy the splendid sights of spring. But now the same plants that I once thought of as friends seemed to be mocking me with the vibrant colors of their rebirth. They surrounded me and dared me to notice how alive they were. I willed myself to block out their taunts and ignore their liveliness. I carefully opened my eyes again. The world was now black and white, with a little gray thrown in for interest.

Just an hour before, my life had been normal. Well, as normal as can be for a fourteen year old and her three siblings who were being raised by their young mother in a very small town. It may not have been "normal" normal, but it was normal to me. Now it was gone.

What was I doing at that moment when my normal was slipping away? I know I was on the school bus, returning from the track meet, but what was I doing? Who was I talking to? Was I laughing at one of my teammate's antics or was I quietly watching the freshly planted fields pass by? Why didn't I get a feeling that something was wrong? I had no idea until we were about two miles from the school. I recognized my older sister, Donna, and her boyfriend as his car met the bus. It did a U-turn and was now directly behind us. My younger sister, Dana, was also on the bus and sat a few rows ahead of me. She turned and looked at me with raised eyebrows. I shrugged my shoulders and we went back to talking to our friends. They must have forgotten something at home, I guessed.

When they followed the bus all the way to the school's front entrance, though, I was a little concerned. I knew they weren't there to give us a ride home. We lived within walking distance and, besides, my sister wasn't that nice.

Dana descended the bus steps and I saw Donna leading her away. They're probably just giving her a ride home. Figures. But then I saw Donna's boyfriend, Dave, waiting for me.

"There's been an accident," he said quickly, without

looking me in the eye.

Was it my mom, stepfather, aunt or a family friend? It couldn't be one of my sisters. They were both standing there.

I looked at him and asked, "Who?"

"David," he said.

I have always believed that when someone says, "I can't imagine…" he is really trying to imagine the situation at hand. In this case, though, I hadn't even considered that harm could come to my younger brother. My beloved brother.

"Is he okay?"

"No."

I didn't stay to hear anymore. I had to get to him. Turning, I started across the schoolyard, headed towards home.

"Diane, wait," Dave called after me, but I didn't look back.

As I approached the two-lane highway that ran through our small town, I saw my friend, Tammy, running towards me. Tears ran down her face as she repeated, "I'm so sorry. I can't believe it. I'm so sorry." She wrapped her arms around me and sobbed on my shoulder. I felt trapped and was annoyed that she was impeding my trip home. I just wanted to get to David. I wrestled myself free and left her standing by the roadside.

Through our large living room window, I recognized many neighbors and my mother's friends sitting on our couches and chairs. It seemed odd to see them all together. Before my parents' divorce, they would socialize with many of the other married neighbors. After the divorce, though, my mother was no longer invited to attend their parties. She often said that married women didn't like divorced women around their husbands. Mom always laughed, rolled her eyes and stated that she wouldn't want any of their husbands anyway. For friends, she had joined forces with the few other divorced or single people in the area. I was certain that, until now, these two different groups of people had never been so close together.

I opened the front door and was almost brought to my knees from the weight of the room. I found it difficult to talk and was only able to ask, "Where is he?"

As if in slow motion, their heads turned towards me. I repeated the question. "Where is he?"

Now, their eyes quickly darted away. For many of them, the carpet was suddenly very interesting.

Finally, a woman's voice said, "Your mother is in her bedroom." I was confused. Why wasn't Mom at the hospital?

I entered her room and quickly asked, "Are we going to the hospital?"

She stared blankly at me. Before she could answer, a neighbor led me from the room.

"Your mother wants you girls to speak to Pastor B. He's in your room."

Why do we have to talk to him? We stopped going to church as a family about seven years ago, after the divorce. Surely he knows that. Besides, why aren't we on our way to the hospital? David must be so frightened. It takes at least a half hour to drive there. We need to leave right now, I thought.

The neighbor noticed my hesitancy.

"Go on," she said, guiding me through the door. "The Pastor's waiting."

Donna and Dana entered shortly thereafter. The three of us sat on my bed, facing him.

Pastor B stood and quietly shut the door. He returned to the edge of Dana's bed and introduced himself. He was fairly new to this town and we had never met. After the introductions, he began telling us about his college roommate. Sadly, his friend had died of a brain tumor. After his friend died, he told us, he had many questions for God.

I had a few questions for God, too. *God, why is this Pastor telling us his life story? If he really wanted to help, he could be driving us to the hospital. Also, God, why can't fourteen year olds drive? Well, legally, anyway. If we could, I'd drive myself to the hospital. I know David must be in a panic by now. I hate the thought of him being alone. Look after him, okay?*

After a short prayer, the Pastor looked at us with anguished eyes and stood to leave. I guess he still missed his friend.

Mom walked in and thanked him for coming. *Finally, we can leave for the hospital.*

Instead, I saw Mom accept a hug from another one of her friends who had just arrived. I heard her say, "He was in the water for forty-five minutes before they found him."

What? I stood up. On shaky knees, I approached her and tried to interrupt their conversation.

"Mom?"

No reply. I know it's rude to interrupt unless it's an emergency. But this was an emergency. I had to know.

"Mom?"

This time, she stopped talking and turned towards me.

"Mom, was David alive when they pulled him out of

the water?" I know that that was a crazy question to ask. Who lives after being submerged for forty-five minutes? Sure, miracles happen, but not around here.

Mom didn't immediately answer my crazy question. After a long pause, she looked at me through weary, swollen eyes and whispered, "No."

No. No. No. No. No. No. No. No. It was the loudest whisper I'd ever heard. It echoed through my head, my heart, and my soul. How could one word be so mean? So devastating? So painful? So life-altering? So final. No.

I took a step towards her, desperately wanting her to wrap her arms around me like a life-vest. I wanted to be told that everything would be okay. To be told that, together, we'd get through this tragedy. I wanted her to hold my head up so that I would not drown in this miserable pool of sorrow.

But she had just watched her youngest child's lifeless body being pulled from a cold, dark pond. Rescuing me was more than she could bear. She gently pushed me away and left the room.

2

Day Two

The sun rose today. I was surprised by its bright, shiny appearance. Not a single cloud in the sky. Out of habit, I had flipped my bedside radio on but quickly shut it off. The morning DJ sounded too cheery; like she didn't have a care in the world.

I heard the neighbors' cars as they left for work. I saw their children walking to school. I even saw the school bus go by. I knew Highway 41, only a short distance from our doorstep, would still stretch out north and south of town.

I heard the ding-ding of someone pulling into the nearby gas station to fill up his tank and I swear I even heard the school bell ring, signaling the start of a new day.

The birds continued to fly overhead and I watched a butterfly flit from flower to flower.

I had expected it all to come to a screeching stop when David died. But, it hadn't

At the very least, I said to myself, *it should be raining.*

My sisters, mother and I were alone. Night had fallen and everyone else had returned to his or her lives. We sat in silence, lost in our own thoughts. My mother looked defeated and I was too dumbfounded to speak.

"I don't know what I'd do if I had lost my David,"

Donna blurted out. She was referring to her boyfriend, David, not our brother.

I slowly looked in her direction, too confused for words. Was she saying that, if there had been a choice, she'd have chosen her David over our brother David? What? She was seventeen; David was nine. That's a lot of years in between, a lot of separation. I knew she was clinging to her boyfriend for comfort during all of this but I still couldn't comprehend her words. I knew that I would have chosen our brother's life over everyone else's, including my own. And right now, especially my own.

I looked at the others. First at Mom, who had almost shut down and was just barely functioning. I saw anger flash across her face, but it quickly faded. She and Donna had a strained relationship even before David died. They were only sixteen years apart and Donna had always been strong-willed. I don't think Mom knew how to handle her most of the time. She let the statement go by without a response. I then looked at Dana, who I had yet to see cry. Wasn't she even upset by this? Where were her tears? Maybe she was thinking that she was glad that it hadn't been Donna who had died. Even though she was closest in age to David, she got along best with Donna. When teams had to be chosen for games, it was always Donna and Dana versus David and me. Still, I wondered, how could she not be crying?

I, on the other hand, couldn't seem to stop crying. I cried as soon as I awoke and realized that my nightmare was really my new life. I cried while I brushed my teeth, while taking a shower, and while getting dressed. Earlier in the day, we had been sitting in the kitchen with some visitors. I was in the corner chair, just listening to their conversation. When they stopped talking for a minute, I burst into tears. I couldn't control myself. Mom just looked at me from across the table. I hung my head and sobbed into my chest. One of the visitors, Karen, approached me and took me by the hand, pulling me to my feet. I blindly followed her outside to the front steps of the porch.

The bright sun had warmed the cement steps and we both sat down. She put her arm around me and stated that she knew how hard this was for me. Since learning of David's death, she was the first adult who held me and told me that we would get through this. I leaned into her and sobbed. For that short time, I didn't feel so alone

Finally, I looked back at Donna. What could I say? Nothing. I went to my room, crawled into bed, and cried myself to sleep.

3

Later That Week

We had the funeral, of course. The days between David's death and the service seemed suspended in time. We had a refrigerator full of casseroles and Jell-O salads that had been delivered by the townspeople, but we could not eat. Instead, we forced them on visitors who dared linger more than five minutes.

"Eat, please," Mom would beg. "Otherwise, it'll all just go to waste."

So, friends who had come to express condolences would stay and eat. In their kindness, they all offered to help in any way they could. But, really, what could they do to help a helpless situation? Since they obviously couldn't raise the dead, they ate.

None of my friends stopped by during this time. Only one of them worked up the courage to call. As soon as I heard her voice, all I could do was cry. I kept telling her how sorry I was to be crying, but she kept saying that it was okay. I finally pulled myself together, thanked her for calling and hung up. I was relieved nobody else called for me.

On one of the days, too, we had to shop for new outfits for the funeral. I usually loved shopping, but under these circumstances, it was a chore. How do you choose something to wear to your brother's funeral? Do you be practical and buy something you might like to wear again? Or do you go with something perfectly cheap and dreadful because you know you'll never be able to look at it again without thinking about the funeral? In the end, I let my aunt decide since it all looked the same to me.

After we all had new outfits, my aunt led us to the boys' section.

"What are we doing?" I asked.

She looked at us and quietly said, "We have to buy a sweater, uh, for David." Something for him to be buried in, is what she meant to say. I wanted to buy him a new sweatshirt instead of a sweater.

Aunt, though, said, "No, that wouldn't be appropriate."

Who knew that even in death there were dress codes? So, we began searching for a sweater to match the pair of dark blue pants and plaid shirt he had planned on wearing to the upcoming graduation parties. After visiting numerous stores and repeating what we needed each time, we finally found one. It was a white cardigan sweater. He would have hated it.

The night before the funeral, we had the wake. All of our relatives from Chicago had arrived in time. All ten of them were staying with us, so my sisters and I were sleeping on the living room floor and quietly fighting for a few minutes to shower in our one bathroom. The up side was that my mother stopped worrying about all of that food going to waste.

The wake, or visitation as some called it, was surreal. My mother, stepfather, sisters and I were allowed to arrive a short time before the funeral home doors were opened to the public. I had never been in a place like that before. I briefly wondered if it was haunted. I mean, so many dead bodies had been prepared and shown there. Who's to say some of the spirits didn't stick around? I knew I wouldn't want to be there alone at night.

The bright sun managed to peek through the crimson velvet curtains that flanked the multiple windows lining the hallway. We followed the gold runner carpet to a room. Beyond the closed doors, I knew, laid my brother. I pinched myself, hoping to end this nightmare. Instead, the funeral home director opened the door. There, in the white child-sized casket we had chosen, laid my brother. *Oh, David. Oh, God. Why? Why?*

I stood back and let the others go first. Okay, now would be an even better time to wake up. *God, are you listening?* No answer.

Now it was my turn. I walked up to the casket. He looked so peaceful. Like he had fallen asleep before I made it to his room to tell him how much I loved him and wished him a good night. Maybe he was the one sleeping. I reached out to touch his cheek and a shiver ran down my spine. His cheek was hard and cold. I hadn't expected that. His cheek was hard and cold, he was wearing that sissy white cardigan and his hair was perfectly combed. Everything was wrong. I slightly messed his hair and walked away. It was time to let the community express their sorrows over our loss.

When I walked by David's casket later, his hair was once again perfectly combed. I messed it up. After I walked away, from the corner of my eye, I saw the funeral director quietly approach the casket, slide a comb from his pocket, and straighten David's hair. Before long, I was back at the casket to tussle his hair again. I even saw my mother do it once. Each time, the funeral director would quietly comb it. This went on all evening.

During the funeral the following day, I found it comforting to be back in the church, although I wished it were under different circumstances. I guess we were still considered members, even though we hadn't attended services in years.

David's best friend, J, was there. He had watched David drown. We learned that David, J, and two other boys had built rafts from wooden pallets. Maybe they wanted to be Tom Sawyer and Huck Finn and set sail on a great adventure. Instead of the mighty Mississippi, they had settled for a spring-fed pond that went nowhere.

David and J were on the first raft, while the other boys were on the second one. The second raft started to sink so those boys jumped onto the first raft. Under the extra weight, the first raft began to sink as well. After all, these rafts were really just re-worked wood pallets. Re-worked, I might add, by nine-year-old boys. I wouldn't have trusted either raft in a bathtub.

As the rafts sank, the boys were plunged into bitter cold water. It was only May, but even in August the pond water was cold. David knew how to swim but the coldness of the water must have shocked him. The three other boys made it to the grassy banks.

I don't remember anything from the actual service. It was all background noise as I stared silently at my little brother lying in that casket. Wreaths of flowers stood on either side. The biggest one had a banner that said, "Son, Brother and Nephew." The other wreath said, "Friend." Obviously, the first one was from our family. The second one was a gift from his fourth grade class. The students had all brought in money to buy a wreath for their classmate's funeral. Vases of flowers and potted plants filled the front of the church. The persistent sun streamed through the stained glass windows and danced across their leaves.

I stared so long and hard at David's body that I swore I saw him take a breath. Hope surged through my veins. Maybe miracles do happen around here. I continued to look but I didn't see it again. Nothing more than wishful thinking. The sun must have gone behind a cloud because the room now seemed a little dimmer. David was still dressed in the outfit from the night before. I guess the dead are given a pass on that dress code rule. He would have hated the sweater but I was glad he had it on. I knew he couldn't feel cold anymore, but I felt better thinking he was properly dressed for where he was going. I guess it is similar to dressing stuffed animals. You know they can't feel the cold, but you do it anyway, just in case.

I took one last look before the lid was closed forever. The funeral director had won. David's hair was perfectly combed.

After the church service, I glanced over at J. His thumb and forefinger were tightly pressed into the corner of his eyes. Like the Little Dutch Boy, he used his fingers to prevent the dam from breaking. How awful it must be to watch your best friend die. I recognized the anguish I had seen days earlier in the Pastor's eyes.

Standing near the church's double-glass doors, I quietly observed my brother's casket being lifted into the back of the hearse. After leaving the church, it would drive right by our house on its way to the cemetery. Upon arriving, the casket would be lowered into the plot Mom and I had chosen a few days earlier. The caretaker had met us at the cemetery and quietly showed us the available spaces. When he showed us one area, he gently mentioned that three spots could be purchased. Mom recoiled from his words as if there were slaps.

"No, no," she stammered, looking at me and then back at him. "I only need one. I only need one."

I silently wished she'd buy at least one more. If I died, I'd want to be buried next to my brother.

We wouldn't be going to the cemetery after the church service. Mom wouldn't allow that part of the funeral to take place. She said that no mother should ever have to watch one of her children being put into the ground.

As the long, dark car pulled away, a slight drizzle escaped the gray skies.

4

We Return to School

We returned to school today, my sisters and I. It was strange not hearing the shower at 6:00 A.M. David had once told our mother that he had to get up at that time because we wouldn't let him in the bathroom. Our house held three teenage girls and one bathroom. There simply wasn't room in that small bathroom for a little brother.

Less than a week remains of the school year, but we had to return for final exams. It's just as well. It's too quiet at home.

I took two Michigan history tests. One was a make-up exam and the other was the final. I flunked both of them. Well, okay, I got a D- on one but only because the teacher felt sorry for me.

He didn't say that, of course, but I could tell. He told me he tried to have me pass both, but he just couldn't do it. He looked relieved when I shrugged my shoulders and said, "It's okay. I didn't study for either test."

That was the first time I'd ever failed an exam.

"He's not dead. He's just away." That's what some of the sympathy cards we received had stated. I memorized the whole poem:

> *I cannot say and I will not say*
> *That he is dead – he is just away!*

17

With a cheery smile,
And a wave of hand,
He has wandered into an unknown land,
And left us dreaming how very fair
It needs must be, since he lingers there,
And you — O you, who the wildest yearn
For the old time step and glad return,
Think of him faring on, as dear,
In the love of There as the love of Here;
Think of him still as the same, I say;
He is not dead — he is just away!
- James Whitcomb Riley

Yep, that's me, wanting that glad return. Maybe he didn't really die. Maybe aliens abducted him and now they're keeping him for their experiments. Wait, no, I don't like the thought of that. Maybe, instead, a childless couple has kidnapped him and convinced him that we're all dead. Yes, that's it. He's been kidnapped. They are taking good care of him. (They really are nice people, after all, except for the kidnapping thing.) I'm sure he misses us desperately. Soon, he'll learn the truth and come home. I can hardly wait.

I wonder, though, how the kidnappers impersonated David's body at the funeral. It looked so real.

The aliens must have helped.

Today was the last day of school. I passed eighth grade. Big deal. After the final bell, the seniors left the parking lot with their music blaring and their horns blasting. Each decibel made my heart ache. How could they be so happy? Don't they care that this small town lost a member less than two weeks ago? Do they even remember? Perhaps they don't. Since we returned to school, not one person has spoken David's name to me. My friends have avoided the subject. Even the teachers haven't said anything. Sure, the history teacher sort of acknowledged it, but never came out and said David's name. My science teacher said that it was good to see me back in school.

But nobody mentioned David. Are they afraid of reminding me that my heart had just been ripped from my body? Are they afraid I'd suddenly remember that a huge part of me had died and was buried in a little country cemetery? Maybe they are afraid I'll start to cry and then what would they do? They should not fear that one. I have no tears left. Perhaps they can't look me in the eye and say his name because they know what I'm in for. My future only looks painful now. I don't know that it ever looked bright but there was hope. There had always been hope.

Now, there's just this pain. It's my new constant companion. I can't see the day when this will go away or when it will all be okay again. It hasn't been that long, but I've already forgotten what I felt like before David died. I must have felt lighter, somehow. What was I worried about before then? What did I fear? Who was I? I don't know. I just know that I'm not that same person anymore. This has changed me but I haven't figured out who the new me will be yet. I have heard the saying that whatever doesn't kill you makes you stronger. Will I be stronger after this? When does after begin? If I don't get stronger, will it kill me? Are those my only choices?

At least the teachers aren't telling me how sorry they are for my loss. If I had heard that one more time at the funeral, I was prepared to scream loud and long. Why do people say that? "I'm sorry." I wanted to start asking, "Why? Did you kill him? Did you watch him drown and do nothing to help? Why are you sorry?" Besides, what was I supposed to say in response? "Thank you," or "Oh, no problem," or, "It's okay?"

I think a more appropriate thing to say would be, "I think it stinks that you have to go through this heart-wrenching experience, especially at such a young age. I know how much you loved your brother. I often saw the two of you playing in your front yard. Sometimes, life just isn't fair."

As the noises from the cars were fading, Donna turned to me and said, "That will be me next year. I can't wait to celebrate my last year of high school."

I guess they do have a right to be happy. But I wonder if I will ever want to celebrate again. I can't imagine that.

5

Summer

I know I should cry or at least feel worse than I do. Mom told me today that my seventeen-year-old stepsister had died. Although she actually died around the same time that David had, Mom postponed telling us. She didn't think we could handle more tragic news.

I had only met my stepsisters five years ago. My biological father was interested in getting to know Donna, Dana and me better, so Mom allowed us to spend a few weeks with him in Illinois during the summer. The first few visits, only Donna and I went because Mom felt Dana was too young to go. Eventually, Dana would make the trips with us. Ironically, after leaving our mother with three young girls to rear alone, he married a woman with three young girls. After getting to know him and seeing the run-down, rodent infested house they all lived in, I knew we had gotten the better deal. He had promised Mom that he wouldn't drink around us, and he didn't. But I realized the hardships that they had were due to his alcoholism. I knew the little that they did have was due to the hard work of his wife.

Regardless of their living conditions, I enjoyed spending time at their house. During the day, I would hang out with the neighbor kids who knew their way around the area. We would often walk to a nearby creek and try our luck at fishing. We never caught anything, but we had enough nibbles to make it exciting. In the evening, all of us girls would retreat to P and D's bedroom. The oldest sister, R, no longer lived at home. They didn't talk about her much, but I think she lived with her boyfriend and seemed to have many problems of her own.

Even though I was closer in age to P, I got along best with D. We liked the same music and agreed on many topics. In spite of her being three years older, she didn't boss me around or treat me like a kid. I loved that about her.

I hadn't seen her in the last two years. After my biological father asked me to stop calling him "Dad," I lost the desire to visit with him. He had suggested that I call him by his nickname, "Slim." I had heard his stepdaughters calling him that and thought it was strange that they didn't call him "Dad." I thought I could, though. After all, he was my father. I was wrong. I stopped calling him "Dad" during that visit, but I never called him "Slim," either. I hadn't returned to his house since then and now, I knew, I never would.

D was gone. She had died of a drug-overdose. I wasn't told if it was accidental or intentional. I guess the troubles in her life didn't make her stronger, but killed her instead. If I wasn't so numb, I knew I'd cry for her but, right now, I couldn't. Any tears that I could even manage to draw from my eyes would've been for David. But that well had finally gone dry.

I'm spending my summer days as a janitor at the school. Donna is also working there. The jobs were offered to students from families of low income. I'm not supposed to know that, but it wasn't hard to figure out when I saw who else was given a job. Donna and I are the only siblings in the program.

We scrub and wax floors, clean desks, wash walls and paint fences. The boys are lucky. They also get to mow the lawn. I don't mind doing any of this other stuff, though. It beats sitting at home all day.

We played basketball during our lunch break today. The head janitor divided us into teams. The game was so fast paced and intense that nobody, including our boss, noticed that we had played past our allotted break time. When he finally looked at the clock, the game abruptly ended. I dribbled the ball off of the court. I was exhausted and sweaty but I felt calm.

After I placed the ball on the rack, guilt washed over me. I hadn't thought about David the entire game. How could that be? For the last two months, thoughts of David occupied every waking moment. Well, almost every moment because I often dreamed of him, too. Now I had just spent forty-five minutes running up and down a basketball court and I hadn't thought of him once. How could I run and play when David is dead? I had probably even laughed at one point, too. I am so sorry, David.

I wonder what it would be like to die. At the funeral, I overheard someone say that drowning is a peaceful way to go. How does anyone really know these things? Besides, I don't think it was peaceful for David. His friends said that he splashed a lot and cried for help. When he was pulled from the water, his eyes and mouth were wide open. It looked like he died screaming.

I sometimes want to scream until I die. I don't want to die, really. I just want to be with David, that's all. I miss everything about him. I miss helping him with his homework. I miss playing catch with him. When I was in the fifth grade, my teacher taught me how to throw a football. I had recently shown David how to do it. We practiced often. He was getting so good at it.

Mostly, though, I miss tucking him in at night.

"You know I love you, don't you?" I'd ask him. Our mother works at night and I wanted him to fall asleep knowing he was wanted and loved.

"Ya, I know," he'd answer.

If I joined him now, we could play catch and I could tuck him in again. We'd skip the homework.

How would I do it? How would I kill myself? I don't have access to a gun, so that option is out. That'd be dreadful, anyway. A man in the next town over killed himself that way. He made a real mess. I don't want anyone to have to scrape my brains off the ceiling.

I could overdose. That's how D had died. Never mind. I hate swallowing pills. I won't even take an aspirin. That won't work.

There are no cliffs around to leap from. The tallest building is the school. I might get hurt jumping from the second story, but I doubt I'd die. What's the point of that?

A train goes through town a couple of times a day. I could curl up on the tracks and wait. No, I couldn't. That would be awful for the engineer. No sense ruining someone else's life.

I could ingest some poison. Ok. Now, where will I get it? I've heard of food poisoning. Would that do it? And, again, how would I get it? Donna's cooking is bad, but it hasn't killed anyone.

I know! I'll starve myself to death. That's it! I'll just stop eating. I don't usually eat breakfast anyway so lunch and dinner shouldn't be a big deal to miss, too.

Well, maybe not. It would take too long and my mom would notice.

Mom. Oh, ya. I don't think she could handle losing another child. When she's not at work, she's asleep on the couch. She closes the curtains and gets angry if we try to open them to let in some light. She has become a mole person. She sleeps all day and works all night. I doubt she'd want to come out of the safety of her dark hole to plan another funeral.

I long to retreat into a dark hole somewhere. When did the process of grieving change? Whatever happened to dressing in black for a year and being banned from social gatherings? I think it would be easier to go back to those rituals.

I'm expected to act as if nothing has happened. If I'm not smiling or talking, everyone wants to know, "What's wrong?" I'll tell you what's wrong. My nine-year-old brother drowned in a cold, dark pond last spring and people expect me to just get on with my life. My mother acts like a mole and none of us even mention David's name anymore. Misery doesn't love company. Misery wants to be left alone to pretend it doesn't exist.

If I don't laugh at a joke, my friends question me. If I do force a laugh, I feel so guilty. How could I possibly find anything funny? My brother is dead. That is not funny.

The only time I am not worried about talking or not talking, smiling or not smiling, and laughing or not laughing is when I have a basketball in my hands. To properly grasp the ball, I have to lay everything else aside. The pain, the anger, the deep sorrow, all of it must

25

be set aside. I've played on the school's basketball team since seventh grade because I've always wanted to. This year I need to be on the team. I need to run sprints until I collapse. I need to practice free throws until my arms ache. I need to draw the ball to my face and get lost in the smell of leather. I need to daydream about the game when school gets too boring. I need to be a part of the team because I don't have the safety net of being banned from social gatherings. Since I am forced to still be an active member of our little town, I need to play basketball.

6

Ninth Grade
Fall

I hate my basketball coach. All he does is yell. Especially at me. I can't be the only one making mistakes. Can I? Of course, I knew he yelled a lot. He was my seventh and eighth grade basketball coach. This year, he's coaching junior varsity. I knew he wouldn't change over the summer, so I am not surprised by his coaching techniques. Today, however, he seemed especially brutal. I ended practice feeling completely humiliated. Does he think I'm not trying? Does he think I throw the ball away or miss shots on purpose? Geez.

I finally finished making my required twenty-five free throws and headed towards the locker room.

"What's the matter?" I heard.

I stopped in front of Coach L and shrugged my shoulders. He was the girls' varsity coach and I knew better than to just walk right by him. He, too, was known as a very vocal coach. If that wasn't intimidating enough, he was also my math teacher.

"Are you upset because your coach yelled at you a lot today?" he asked.

I knew better than to shrug this time. I nodded my head and quietly said, "Yes."

"You know he only yells because he cares, don't you?"

I shrugged my shoulders again. I couldn't help it. I was afraid my voice would betray me, and then he'd know how close I was to tears. In math class, this type of behavior would have been considered very disrespectful.

Instead of responding in anger, he gently advised, "You should be upset if he stops yelling." He paused. "Because that would mean he's given up on you."

Oh. So, being yelled at is a good thing? I still didn't like it, but I did feel less humiliated. I met Coach L's gaze and said, "Okay."

I guess I don't hate my coach.

From the corner of my eye, I saw the color orange. Basketball orange.

I wonder why nobody talks to us about David. The whole town knows about him. The whole town knew him. Yet, it's as though he never existed. Not just ceased to exist, but never even existed. Is everyone afraid they'll remind me of him? Don't they know I think of him constantly? I have to remain vigilant; otherwise, he'll be forgotten.

Perhaps they've already done so. No, I can't believe that. Besides, people in small towns never forget anything.

I wish someone would just say his name to me. I want to hear a funny story about him. Well, maybe not funny, not yet. A nice story would be, well, nice. Maybe someone could tell me a story about him doing something for someone else.

I want some proof that he was here. I want proof that he existed. Even his bedroom is gone. I came home from school one day and all of his belongings had been replaced with Donna's. Before he "wandered into an unknown land," David had his own room while Donna and Mom shared a room. Dana and I shared the only other bedroom. Mom had been saving to have part of the garage converted to a room for Donna. Those plans are no longer necessary. The saved money was used for my brother's funeral.

I was shocked to see that David no longer had a bedroom. I figured he would be very angry when he finally escaped from those kidnappers and made it home to us. How would my mother explain that she had believed he was dead? Only I would be able to say that I never gave up hope for his eventual return.

I no longer see any of David's clothes or other belongings. I don't know what Mom did with them. I'm afraid to ask.

Unfortunately, I do know what she did to his dog, TJ. She said that she couldn't listen to him anymore. Since David died, TJ just laid near his doghouse. He had no interest in food and barely ate enough to remain alive. Every night, as we all lay in our beds waiting to escape through sleep, he'd begin a slow, mournful whimper. His house was positioned near my bedroom window and his cries reverberated throughout our bedrooms. We moved his house further away from ours, but that seemed to provoke louder and more insistent cries. How do you console a dog? Do you lie and say, "David's not dead, he's just away?"

Again, I came home from school, and TJ was gone. I started having second thoughts about going to school.

"Where's TJ?" I asked, even though I knew the answer.

"I had a friend take him to a farm," Mom replied.

"Which one? I want him back."

"It's too late." She turned and left the room.

That meant that he had been taken to a field somewhere

and shot. In that moment, my heart filled with rage towards my mother. How could she kill the last living thing connected to David? First his room, then his belongings, and now his dog? Could she have at least consulted the rest of us? It was heartbreaking to listen to him cry at night, but I didn't want him dead. She's as bad as everyone else in this town, wanting to act as if David never existed. Well, he did exist. I know he did. Didn't he?

All we are is dust in the wind. These are lines from a song performed by the group Kansas. It was David's favorite song when he died. I wonder if he had a feeling that something was going to happen to him. Why else would a nine year old beg his mother to buy him a song about death and dying?

The song now haunts me. When I hear it on the radio, a wave of grief washes over my body. I want it to stop; yet, I can't bear to turn it off. It is a reminder of David, the only apparent one these days. The songs message is about accepting death as a part of life.

Mom's favorite part is about not hanging on, because nothing lasts forever, and no matter how much money you have, it won't buy another minute for you or anyone else.

Death: the great equalizer. In this case, it wouldn't matter if she were educated, had a decent job, lived in a fancy house, or drove an expensive car. This time, she can't be blamed for not being smart enough, rich enough, or good enough. I guess that somehow makes her feel better.

I don't have a favorite line. I can recognize the song in

the first few opening notes and I know the lyrics by heart. Still, when it plays on the radio, I am not analyzing the words and their meanings. I concentrate only on breathing until the song ends.

My friends know that David loved this song. If it plays while we are all together, they, too, get quiet. We never discuss the song, or the stillness that ensues when it plays, but I appreciate their awareness. It would hurt if they just kept talking and laughing as David's song was being aired.

I entered our house and immediately threw my gym bag at the sofa.

"What's your problem?" Dana asked.

"You won't believe what I heard at school today," I started. "D told me
that his cousin watched David drown."

"Ya, I've heard that, too," she said quietly. "I guess he heard the other boys calling for help and went to his window to see what all the commotion was about."

"What? You knew that? I can't believe you're so calm about it. I'm furious that he didn't try to save him."

"Uh, you do remember that he had a broken leg at the time, don't you?"

"So!" I was yelling now. "If I had a broken leg, even two broken legs, I never would have just watched someone drown from the window of my house."

"How was he supposed to get from his house to the pond?"

"I don't know. He could've hopped or even rolled. He could've at least tried."

"I think he would've been stupid to try," Dana reasoned. "He had a broken leg. His leg was in a cast. He had to use crutches just to get around. He probably would've drowned, too, if he had tried to save our brother." She was speaking very slowly, as if she were talking to a crazy person. The look on her face clearly indicated that she thought I had lost my mind.

"I don't care," I screamed in reply. "I would've jumped in after him. If I had been there I would've saved him. I should have been there. Why did I go to that dumb track meet? If I had been here, maybe we would've played catch together or something and then he wouldn't have gone to the stupid pond in the first place. I should've been here. I would've saved him."

"No," Dana said, "You probably would've drowned, too."

"I don't care!" I was still screaming. "At least I would've tried. Don't you even care that David died?"

"I care."

"I haven't even seen you cry. You didn't cry the day he died, you didn't cry at the funeral, and I haven't seen you cry since. If you care, why haven't you cried?"

I was truly confused. I had learned that people grieved differently, but to not even cry? I had cried until I had no tears left. I didn't know not crying was even a possibility.

"I can't cry."

"What do you mean you can't cry?" I was still angry and not at all understanding.

She looked me in the eye. "I've tried to cry. I wish I could cry. But, I can't."

Pastor B's three-year old son, Jonathan, has died. I heard about it in English class when one of my classmates asked our teacher why his mother had gone home early. She worked as the school's secretary and her absence had been noticed.

Mr. Mortenson didn't immediately answer. He looked over at me and then towards the rest of the class. I heard him softly say, "Well, you're all going to find out anyway." Then, "Pastor B's young son has died. He had been ill for the past month, but nobody's sure yet what caused him to die."

For once, I was thankful to be sitting in the front corner of the classroom. I could feel that all eyes were on my back and expectancy hung in the air. Oh, how I wanted to get up and bolt out the door. Is that what was expected of me? Where would I go, though? Home? The bathroom? Should I go hide in the locker room until practice this afternoon? But what would be the point, really? I couldn't escape the news. Instead, I stayed, sat very still, stared at the door and waited for the teacher to start the lesson.

How can God take a Pastor's son? Shouldn't he be immune from such awful things? I mean, he preaches God's word. I didn't understand David's death and I certainly didn't understand Jonathan's, either. Everything seemed to be slipping away.

Mom and I went to the funeral at the church, only four and a half months after David's. Mom didn't want to go alone, and neither Donna nor Dana would go with her. So, I did. We stopped at the front door, gathered our courage, and went through the entrance. As we rounded the corner and proceeded towards the steps leading to the sanctuary, we suddenly stopped. There was Jonathan's casket, in the narthex at the top of the stairs. We both had expected it to be at the front of the church, like David's had been. We gathered our courage once again, and waited our turn to express our condolences to Pastor and Mrs. B. I didn't know what to say and I knew I didn't want to say the "wrong" thing. I couldn't bear to say the old standby, "I'm sorry," since that had so annoyed me at David's funeral. So, I hung back and waited for Mom to finish. When she was done, I joined her at the casket.

"Oh, he's so young," I whispered. His outfit was very similar to the one David had worn. Jonathan even had on a white cardigan. I noticed a few toys by his side, just like with David. We had placed a monkey in David's casket. When he was much younger, Mom and he had been in a store. They were walking past the toy section when David had spotted the monkey. Without a word, he picked up the monkey, kissed its head, hugged it, and set it back on the shelf. Even though she couldn't really afford to do so, Mom bought it for him. It had been his constant companion for years. Before his death, we all knew he still slept with that monkey, even though he denied it.

Under Jonathan's folded arm, I noticed a Bible. Uh-oh. We hadn't included one with David. Was that the ticket into Heaven? I hoped God would forgive our oversight.

As Pastor B preached at his son's funeral, I marveled at his strength. I couldn't stop crying for days after David's death, and here he was offering God's words as a way to comfort the townspeople who had shown up for the funeral. He told us that the Lord has many rooms in his house, and he would one day meet Jonathan there.

I imagined David in one of those rooms, too. I prayed to God every night, but I had also begun to speak to

David on a regular basis. Never aloud, of course, since I didn't want anyone to think I was crazy.

"David, look after Jonathan," I told him in my head. "Show him around, please. Let him play with you and TJ." Ever since our dog was shot, I liked to picture him in Heaven with David.

As we walked to the car after the service, I asked Mom what she had said to the Pastor.

"Nothing," she replied. "There was nothing to say, so I just held his hand."

7

Winter

The holiday season is fast approaching. Oh, joy.
Years past, we would have Thanksgiving with
Aunt, my stepfather's sister. My mother was always
invited to attend. Some years she would, and some years
she wouldn't. Some years, too, she'd come and have a little too much to drink and get into heated debates with
Aunt, who also had a little too much to drink. One year,
for our entertainment, they discussed legal abortion. My
mother, who had given birth to the three of us girls
before she turned twenty-one, was strongly in favor of it.
My aunt, who had never had children, strongly opposed
it. I was too young and too confused to really decide
with whom I agreed. They both made strong -and loud-
arguments. I was left with a vague feeling, though, that I
probably wouldn't have been sitting there if it had been
legal when Mom was pregnant with me. My sisters probably wouldn't have been there, either. It was ironic that
the only child she planned on having, my brother, was
taken from her.

I doubt there will be any arguments this year. The fight
has drained from Mom. She still goes to work everyday,
pays the bills, grocery shops and performs all of the
other mundane tasks of living. But, I know she's just here
because we are still here. Just like I wouldn't take my
own life for fear of hurting her, she isn't going to take
hers for fear of hurting us. Life has kicked her down a
few times already.

She ran away from home with my biological father when she was just fifteen. She doesn't talk much about it, but I know her home life wasn't good. Why else would she run away? When she turned twenty-two, she figured out that he wasn't going to stop drinking and leaving her alone with three young children for weeks at a time so she divorced him. She eventually married my stepfather and, together, they had David. My brother, please don't call him my half-brother—he was whole to me—was born when she was twenty-four. After almost four years of marriage, they divorced and she was on her own to rear four children. No education, no job, and no job skills. Still, each time, she managed to get back up. Now, she was still standing, but just barely.

Christmas. What a disaster. It used to be my favorite holiday. I especially loved shopping for the tree. The past few years we had met my stepfather at a lot in a nearby town. My siblings and I would all yell, "There it is!" when we'd round the corner and see the little lights illuminating the lot where the evergreen trees were sold. Louis would be waiting on the corner. He always looked so warm and comfortable outside, regardless of what the thermometer read.

Mom hated the cold so she'd sit in the car with the engine running and the heat blasting through the vents. The rest of us would walk around stomping our feet and breathing on our gloved hands, trying to stay warm. Oh, how I loved the smell of those trees. Even in the cold, the smell permeated the air and filled my nostrils with such a clean, fresh scent. I would stand as close as I possibly could without getting my eyes poked out, and inhale every tree that we stopped to admire.

"I like this one," I said, hopefully.

"You say that about every tree," Donna retorted.

"Why are you smelling the trees?" Dana asked.

Louis chuckled and asked if we knew where David was.

"I'm over here, Dad," a tree from the other aisle seemed to answer.

We'd make our way over and there would be David, in front of the perfect tree. Every year, we would declare his the best tree on the lot, pay for it, and watch expectantly as it was tied to the roof of our car. With that wonderful chore accomplished, we'd head to the concession stand where we knew Louis would treat us to the world's best tasting hot cocoa. One year, I had seen the owners preparing the drink. It was from a mix. In fact, it was the same brand that we had at home. But theirs always tasted so much better in that cold, heavily scented, dimly lit tree lot.

This year we went to the tree lot because we were all trying so hard not to let David's death kill us, too. That whole survival, make-you-stronger thing, I guess. As we approached the lot, we saw Louis standing there. He looked cold. My sisters and I got out while Mom stayed in the heated car. I was glad to see that not everything had changed. The lot seemed different, somehow. The trees were there, of course, but they all looked the same. I don't remember whether or not they had any kind of scent. We walked around, not even feeling the cold this year, and commented on the trees.

"This would work."

"Ya, so would this one."

"I like this one," Dana said.

We all looked at her tree and approved. She was the youngest now, so she got to pick.

After the tree was securely attached to the car's roof, Louis offered to treat us to hot cocoa.

"I need to get home and study for a test," Donna offered.

"I'm tired," Dana explained.

"I can have some at home. It's just from a mix, anyway." I replied.

Louis looked relieved. "Okay, then. Drive safely."

When we arrived home, we helped Mom remove the tree from our car. Usually, we'd want to know when she was going to put the lights and garland on so we could hang the ornaments. Instead, we leaned the tree in the corner of the garage, set it free from its bindings and went inside the house.

A few days later, Mom had put the tree up while we were at school. Now, it was our turn. She had left the box of ornaments on the chair and it dared us to open it when we were all home.

Donna lifted the lid and started passing out the red, blue, and silver bulbs. Just like that. When we finished hanging the ornaments, we stood back and looked at the tree. It was top heavy. It had always been David's job to decorate the lowest branches. Without thinking, we had left them for him. Only the lights and the garland adorned the lower part of our Christmas tree. In a strange way, it seemed appropriate but, oh, so wrong.

None of us moved to correct our oversight. Donna gathered up the remaining hangers, the tinsel we had decided not to use and the empty ornament box. She threw them in a closet where they would continue to be in the way until the tree came down, the ornaments were once again stored in the attic and this holiday finally over.

As the week progressed, the ornaments slowly migrated south. Every time I was alone with the tree, I moved one or two to a lower branch. I would only do a few at a time, hoping nobody would notice. My sisters must have had the same idea. By Christmas morning, the tree was masquerading as normal.

We waited until after an early dinner to open gifts. We couldn't put it off any longer. Louis, Aunt, and Grandma were all gathered in the living room. I offered to help Mom with the dishes. She saw right through me and waved me into the living room.

"We'll do the dishes later," she said. She walked towards the tree as if she were walking towards a firing squad. I didn't hear it, but I saw her body take a deep breath of air.

When Donna had finished passing out the gifts, we silently stared at the wrapped packages before us. They all looked the same to me.

Dana looked up from her pile. All eyes were on her. The youngest always opened a gift first.

"Oh." She looked embarrassed.

After opening her gift and thanking Mom, she looked at me. Perplexed, I looked around the room and noticed everyone's gaze. We had always watched David open all of his gifts before the rest of us took turns opening ours. My brother wasn't spoiled by this deference and none of us girls minded. It was so wonderful watching him tear the brightly colored paper from his packages while listening to his excited yelps of joy. Last year, he had received that train set he so badly wanted. We all laughed as he grinned from ear to ear. He had played with it all day, even falling asleep as the train chugged along the oval track inches from his head. Christmas was always a financial struggle for Mom, but she had managed to make David's perfect.

Remembering the noise of previous years, I was struck with the quietness of this one.

Don't do it, I told myself. *Please don't cry. Just open your gift and let all eyes move over to Donna. Don't cry, don't cry, don't cry.*

I started crying. I couldn't help it. We were all pretending that everything was normal. Even the tree was in on it. Why were we doing this? Who were we kidding? Ourselves? Surely not. We weren't joking with each other, or laughing, or smiling. Mom and Aunt weren't making any effort to entertain the rest of us with some controversial topic. In fact, they were actually being cordial to each other. Everything was wrong. I wanted the noise, the teasing, and the arguments. Mostly, though, I wanted David. I wanted David.

The dam had broken and I started to sob. Not just the eyes watering, whimpering softly kind of crying, but the real kind of sobbing. The blurry eyes, runny nose, gasping for breaths sobbing.

Nobody moved. It was if we were all actors in a play and I had uttered the wrong line. To make matters worse, my line was so wrong the others couldn't go on because the play no longer made any sense. We would have to close the curtain and listen to the audience leaving. Except that this wasn't a play, of course, and the only one who left the performance was my mother.

Aunt moved next to me.

"Come on, Dia, don't cry," she said.

Too late, I thought, as the sobbing continued.

The packages remained untouched, the dishes were finished, Louis, Aunt and Grandma had left, and the tree was unplugged for the year. Christmas was over.

It's the start of a new year. Our family has never been big on New Year's resolutions, and this year's no different. Our collective resolution is survival. We're not interested in bettering ourselves or saving the world. We'll settle for survival. We don't even care if it makes us stronger or not.

My survival will be a little more difficult now that basketball season has ended. The boys' season has started so that will allow for some diversion. But watching is not the same as playing and I already miss the focus the game demands. Our driveway is covered in packed snow so practicing at home is out. Our school does have an open gym policy on Saturdays, though, so I usually walk over there to shoot around for a few hours. I'm careful not to go too early. The elementary boys and girls play their games Saturday mornings and I'm just not ready to watch David's classmates continue on with their young lives. I loved going last year, however, when David was playing. During one game, his shorts were too big and they kept slipping down his backside as he ran up and down the court. He didn't care. He just held his shorts with one hand and dribbled with the other. Mom finally located a safety pin in the crowd and convinced the coach to call a time-out so she could pin his shorts tighter. He didn't want to come off the court and kept telling her that it was fine. She kept demanding that he come to her so she could pin his shorts. Neither would give in, much to the amusement of the crowd. His coach eventually intervened, David came off the court, stood still while his mother pinned his shorts, and then returned to his position. It took a few more minutes before his deeply reddened face returned to the normal flushed hue of an athlete.

My sisters and I also enjoy the rousing games of basketball we have at the DeTemple's house. Mom and Bill have been friends for a few years now. We love having him to dinner and challenging him to taco eating contests. Every time, he matches our tacos one to one, until we grab our stomachs, throw our heads back, and moan our surrender. He'll then eat at least three more tacos, calling us wimps and daring us to eat another between bites.

Bill lost a leg in the Vietnam War when he stepped on a land mine and has lived with his parents since finishing rehabilitation. He has many brothers and sisters, most of them married with children of their own. In fact, his sister Karen was the one who sat with me on our porch the day after David had died. We are often included in their Sunday afternoon dinners and absolutely love going to their house. The only family we have in the area is on my stepfather's side and Mom doesn't always want to spend time with them. She lets us visit whenever we want but she seldom comes along. When we go to Bill's, we all go as a family.

Their home is always alive with action. Children of all ages are scattered throughout the main level, playing games or coloring. Some are getting their snow gear on to go outside, while others have just come back in and are taking theirs off. There's a lot of, "Have you seen my hat? How about my gloves?" When all are dressed, there is always the one who says, "I have to go to the bathroom!" The ones who have come back inside are shedding their boots, jackets, hats and gloves and jockeying for position next to the wood stove. The chaos is wonderful.

Sometime before dinner, Bill will suggest a game of basketball. The first time he did this, I thought he was crazy. I looked at him, looked out the window at the two feet of snow on the ground, and then looked back at him. Surely, he was joking. He saw my puzzled expression and laughed. "We play in the barn's loft," he explained.

"One of these days, that loft is going to collapse with all of you running around up there," warned his mother.

That made me even more intrigued. I grabbed my jacket and followed the group out the door towards the shoveled path that led to the barn. Once inside, someone flicked on the lights in the loft. Still on the bottom floor, I could see the outlines of the old farm equipment stored in the barn. There were no live animals living here, except for the mice and the cats that kept them in control, but the rusted tractors and plows had stories to tell. How many years had that equipment been used to work the fields and crops that would then be sold to feed this family? How many times had Bill's Dad climbed atop that tractor and driven it around the field in all kinds of weather? The equipment seemed to be hibernating until spring, when it would be coaxed awake once again.

I followed the others up the ladder and was shocked

by the size of the court. It spanned two-thirds of the barn and offered plenty of playing room. The remaining third was used to store long forgotten boxes. There were a few chairs scattered around and we threw our jackets on them. It was cold in the loft, but nobody seemed to mind. Once we started playing, we knew we'd heat up.

We divided into teams and started the game. I wondered how Bill was going to play, with only one leg and all. He wore a prosthetic, but still moved a little awkwardly. I shouldn't have worried. He out played and out shot all of us, to include his brothers who showed him no mercy. Of course, none of them really followed the rules of basketball. They thought it was funny when one of them would pin our arms to our sides, forcing us to duck or risk being hit in the head by the pass headed our way. They also found it hilarious to tickle an opponent in the middle of a jump shot. My sisters and I soon caught on to this new way to play basketball. We all teased, laughed and undeniably cheated until we heard the ringing of the cowbell.

"Dinner's ready. We better go. Ma doesn't ring that bell more than once and she doesn't like her food getting cold," Bill said. We all grabbed our jackets, scrambled down the ladder and headed towards the warm yellow glow shining through the kitchen windows.

8

Second Spring

I t's been one year since David died. It's so unfair. I hate
watching the news for fear that I will be informed of
some child's neglect or abuse. Why would God take
away David, who was deeply loved and wanted, but
leave these other unwanted children on Earth? It doesn't
make any sense to me. There are children all over the
world who are enduring horrendous situations, yet they
are forced to live. My brother, who had a good life, had
his end early. Why? And what about the monsters who
neglect or abuse these children? Why do they get to live?
God should wipe them out and send them directly to,
well, you-know-where.

I'm tired of people saying, "God has a plan." How
could any plan involve the death of an innocent boy?
Maybe God looked away for a minute and David slipped
through the cracks. How can we be sure that God does-
n't need a break every now and then, too? It has to be tir-
ing to be "on-call" all day, every day. I don't know everything there is to know about God, in fact, I know very
little. But the God that I want to believe in doesn't kill
children as part of His plan.

I also can't take it when someone says, "Everything
happens for a reason." Really? There's a reason for the
drowning of a nine-year old child? What could that possibly be? Too many nine-year olds in the world? Or was
it to test the rest of us? Not just our family, but David's
friends, too? Why do other nine- and ten-year-old boys

need to be tested? What could be the reason for having a boy watch his best friend drown? How will he ever recover from that? What if it doesn't make him stronger, but breaks him instead? Poor J. I know he avoids us at school. I've seen him turn and run whenever he sees me. I wish I could tell him that we don't blame him. We never have. We were all thankful that nobody else lost his life that day. It could have easily been a double tragedy. Mom tried to see J the day after the drowning, but his mother wouldn't let her talk to him. I don't know if she thought my mom was going to accuse him of leaving his friend to die or somehow blame him, but that was never her intent. She wanted J to know that he would always have a special place in our hearts and how much David truly enjoyed his friendship. Mom left David's clock radio for J. We don't know if he ever received it.

I wish I could tell J all of this. But, I'd have to catch him first and that just seems like too much work.

The lilacs are in bloom. Back when things were normal, I would often duck into the bushes, close my eyes, and inhale the heavily scented air. I could hear the bees buzzing from flower to flower, but it never bothered me. If I sat real still, they left me alone. Before leaving, I would snap one blossom off so that I could continue inhaling the heavenly scent as I went on my way. No lilac scented perfume, drawer liner or air freshener would ever come close to this flower's original fragrance.

When I didn't have the blossom held up to my nose, I would admire its delicate flowers. Looking at lilac bushes from afar, it looks like one big blossom, but up close, it's easy to see that it is really made up of individual pieces. I appreciated how all of the little purple flowers worked together to create something so beautiful. Since the blossoms didn't last all summer, it made them even more special. I briefly wondered if I'd ever care about such things again.

Before normal ended, I'd take an alternate way to school so I could walk past the bushes that line the town's cemetery. It's about one hundred yards from our driveway and the bushes surround the area, so it's never seemed creepy to me. In fact, I used to cut through the cemetery on my way to the store or the post office, but I no longer do that. After David's death, I started paying attention to the names and dates on the headstones. Some people really got to live long lives, but there were enough markers to identify babies or young children that I didn't want to walk through it anymore.

Besides, I spend a lot of time at the cemetery where David is buried. It's a little more than a mile away and I often ride my bike there. The plots are taken care of by someone from the church we never attend. Except for all the dead people, it could be considered a lovely spot, since it is in the country and surrounded by mature trees. Needless to say, it's also very quiet.

I ride directly to David's grave. I don't care to read anyone else's birth and death dates. I already know that he died way too young. I don't have to have it rubbed in my face. After I dismount my bike and put the kickstand in place, I walk into the woods and look for a few wild flowers. I pick a small bouquet, then approach David's grave and put the flowers on his headstone. Often, there is a lone flower already next to his name. We don't know who is leaving these flowers and everyone we've asked denies it. It comforts me, though, because it's proof that not everyone has forgotten about my brother.

I imagine David sitting at the head of his grave, so I sit on the ground at the foot of the plot. I am alone, so I don't worry about anyone seeing me talking to a block of granite. I wouldn't care if anyone saw me, anyway. I have the same one-sided conversation every time. First, I tell him how much I miss him and how much I still love him. Then, I assure him that I will always love him. I sometimes tell him about what's going on at home, but not always. I somehow feel that he already knows all of that, so I don't want to bore him. Mostly, the conversation focuses on how much I miss him. Since there is never a verbal reply, I then just sit with him. When a gentle wind blows through the treetops, I imagine it's him.

"I miss you, too," he whispers.

9

Second Summer

I'm spending the summer working at the school again. Donna has graduated and has a job elsewhere. It's the same duties as last year with a few different employees. There are less than 300 students in our K-12 school so, of course, we all know each other.

After last summer, I was hired to work during the school year, too. It was a little challenging during basketball season, but I made it work. My boss let me clean my assigned rooms after practice, so that was a big help. When I had away games and didn't have time to get them clean, I would ask another student employee to cover for me. Then, at some future date, I would make it up to her and clean her assigned rooms.

I'm thankful I have something to do during the long summer days. After work, I ride to the cemetery or I shoot baskets in the driveway until my arms ache.

Ever since David died, I've longed to know if he is okay. My need to know became even more dire after I had overheard a conversation between Donna and Mom. While taking classes to convert to Catholicism, Donna struggled with a few beliefs. One, in particular, had to do with baptism. She was told that if a non-baptized person dies, he might not go to Hell, but he won't make it to Heaven, either. Even a child who had absolutely no say in the matter, would not make it to Heaven to be with God. That seemed cruel to her. It was very unsettling to me. I thought Jesus loved the little children. David hadn't been baptized but how could he not be in Heaven? Did Jesus only love the baptized children? If David wasn't in Heaven, where was he then?

I wonder if having a deeper faith in God would make this loss easier. Why do some religions believe that a non-baptized child would be welcomed into Heaven and others don't? Isn't it the same God, regardless of the religion? I wasn't even sure where our religion stood on this issue. I hadn't been to church in a long time.

Even after my mom's divorce from my stepfather, I had continued going to services. Up until then, we had all been active members of that small town church. We kids went to Sunday school, participated in the children's choir and plays, and Mom could always be counted on to bring a casserole or dessert to any scheduled pot-luck dinner. But Mom stopped going after three board members of the congregation dropped by our house one evening. When they learned that she and my stepfather had filed for divorce, they stopped by for a little visit.

These men who stood on our doorstep represented the church. Mom was struggling to get by and, perhaps, believed the church would rally around her and give a helping hand, if need be. Isn't that what churches are supposed to do? She didn't like asking for help, but she was an uneducated, unemployed, twenty-something year old woman residing in a small town with few job opportunities. But these men were business owners. Perhaps one of them would offer her a much-needed job.

Not long before, she was living her dream. She had a

husband, a nice house, and four healthy children. She was working on her high school diploma. She wanted nothing else. Now, she was completely on her own, trying to make sense of the direction her life had suddenly taken. Her nearest relatives were six hours away and would only help if she moved to be near them. Since she didn't consider that to be an option, she saw our church as a lifeline that she desperately needed.

Mom welcomed the men in and offered to make coffee. They looked uncomfortable as they declined. They looked even more uncomfortable as they noticed the four of us children nearby. Mom shooed us to our rooms. Apparently, they got right to the point after we had left because we soon heard our mother asking them to leave.

They hadn't come to offer a job or even emotional support. They had come to inform her that they didn't approve of her lifestyle and were considering revoking her church membership. She asked if that would mean that ours would be revoked, as well. When she was told that it wouldn't, she told them to do whatever they wanted to do and, in the meantime, get out of her house. They were lucky she hadn't chased them out with the rolling pin she kept by the back door in case my stepfather showed up uninvited.

After we heard the door slam and their vehicle leave our driveway, we ventured back to the kitchen. Mom sat at the table, visibly shaken as she tried to light her cigarette. Donna took the lighter and lit it for her. She inhaled deeply and held it longer than usual. She exhaled the smoke in a long tired sigh.

She looked at us. "I never wanted this to happen," she angrily began. "I never would've married him if I had known this would happen. We would have stayed in that run-down trailer, out in the middle of nowhere. Do they think I asked for this?"

She took another drag from her cigarette. We stood watching her until she snubbed the butt out in the ashtray. She turned to us again and when she spoke there was no anger.

"Don't think for a minute any of this is your fault. None of you did anything wrong. Do you understand?" She didn't wait for an answer. "You did nothing wrong."

Mom gave up on the church that day. None of us attended services for a long time, but I found myself missing the comfort that it had provided. Mom didn't say anything when I started going to church every Sunday. It wasn't far away and I never minded the walk. I especially enjoyed Sunday school and had set my sights on earning a brand new Bible. I had seen the Bibles presented to the other children after they had recited the Twenty-third Psalm. I knew I could learn it, too. I was nervous about repeating it in front of the other children, but I knew the Sunday school teacher would help if I got a little stuck. I had seen her help the others when they confused a word or two.

Before the other children arrived, I told her that I was ready to recite the passage. She heard me because she said, "Okay." It was hard to concentrate on the lesson because I knew that when we finished discussing it, she would turn to me and ask if I had anything to share. That's what she had done with the others. I was confused when she went from the discussion onto the coloring activity. Too shy to remind her, I picked up the color in front of me and got busy. After many of the other children had already left with their parents, she turned to me and asked, "Are you ready?" No fanfare, no big deal would be made about my earning a Bible. I was disappointed, but I still wanted that Bible.

"The Lord is my Shepherd, I shall not want, He maketh me to lie down in green pastures...." I got half way through and stumbled on a few of the words. I expected her help, like she had done for the others. Instead, she only stared at me. Fine. I started over. When I finished, I knew I had said it perfectly and she would have to give me a Bible.

"I don't have time to sign one today," she said. "I'll give it to you next week." After the next week's class, she handed it to me without a word. I eagerly accepted it and proudly carried it home. I was pleased to see my name written next to the "Presented to" spot but wished I could scribble out her name in the "Presented by" area.

I showed Mom my Bible but didn't tell her about the teacher. She already didn't like this woman and there was no sense in making it worse. We had to see her every time we shopped at the small grocery store in town. Some people would drive to one of the bigger stores thirty miles away to save a few dollars, but Mom never did. "We have to support the people who live in this town," she'd explain to us. She bought gas from the local station for the same reason.

She didn't like having to deal with this woman, though, who worked as a cashier at the store. After the divorce, Mom had to use food stamps to help keep us fed. She hated using them, but what choice did she have? We only bought the basics and never expensive items with the food stamps. Still, we'd get dirty looks from this woman whenever we had to use them. She took them from my mother's outstretched hand as if they were somehow dirty. As if we were somehow dirty.

"She should try paying attention in church," Mom would say as we hauled the groceries out to the car. Not long afterwards, Mom stopped accepting food stamps. She said that she wasn't saving enough money by using them to make it worthwhile. I was relieved because we were all tired of the humiliation that clung to those pieces of paper.

Once I had earned the Bible, I decided not to attend Sunday school. Instead, I would stay and listen to the sermon, while the other children went downstairs for their weekly lesson. Nobody seemed to mind that I stayed and listened or that I was always by myself at church. In fact, one Sunday the pastor even told a story about a young girl whom he saw walking to church most Sundays, in all kinds of weather. My face reddened because I was certain he was talking about me. As we were filing out after the service, a family that lived further down our road offered me a ride home. I gladly accepted. When they offered to start driving me to church, I gladly accepted that, too. Now I wouldn't have to walk in by myself.

Mom no longer believed in churches but she did believe in the basic tenets of religion. I often saw her give clothes, small appliances and even food to those in town who had even less than we did. Those people received government assistance, too, but Mom also worked so we had a little more. Between working and going to school, she wasn't often home but she did keep us warm, clothed and fed.

Through it all, I think she still wanted to believe in God. After David died, however, she received a disturbing card in the mail. We had received many condolence cards and most contained expressions of sorrow and financial assistance to help cover the expenses of a funeral. People in small towns are great that way. On a daily basis, they might annoy you with their petty gossip but in times of need, they are right there to help in anyway possible. Well, most of them. This one particular person had sent a card that only held an admonition. The sender had informed my mother that she was being punished because God did not approve of her lifestyle. Mom threw it in the trash and I'm afraid her tenuous belief in God followed.

Unfortunately, sometime between the divorce and David's death, I had stopped attending church. I had gone from attending every Sunday and many of the youth activities, to just participating in the activities. Increasingly, though, I was feeling like I wasn't fitting in. My shyness kept me on the edge of most groups, even in school. I always did better one-on-one or in small groups. Only when I played basketball did I feel comfortable in a large group. I eventually found it easier not to attend the activities than to go and pretend to be comfortable.

Now David was gone and I wished I had a stronger faith in God to guide me through this. I had so many questions but no answers. I tried to read that Bible I had received years ago but couldn't make sense of the language. And now I was hearing that David might not be in Heaven. I was no longer sure of the one thing I thought I knew for sure.

I would search for the answers in my sleep. In dreams, I would see him, alive and well, playing with his friends. I would watch him and talk to him, yet somehow feel that it was wrong. I knew he shouldn't be there. But, I didn't care. I was relieved to know that, at least in my dreams, he was okay.

Unfortunately, the dreams had stopped after a deeply disturbing nightmare. I had been peering into an old stone wishing well, asking to see David. The water started churning into a whirlpool and, instead of David's face, I saw the face of the Devil. He was laughing.

10

Tenth Grade
Second Fall

I stared into the darkness as my teammates streamed off the bus. We often stopped at a fast-food place on our way home from out-of-town basketball games, and this time was no different. The noise followed them into the restaurant and I sat alone in the back of the bus. I noticed Coach walking towards me.

During the game, one of the other players fell on me as I was falling. She ended up landing on my shoulders and seemed to compact my spine. I lay on the floor as the game was stopped, both teams stood a short distance away, and Coach ran to my side. I felt paralyzed and was truly afraid to move.

Two years before, I had injured my back while practicing the high jump for track. After clearing the bar, I landed incorrectly on the mat. Instantly, I felt a twinge of pain. Within a few months, I was in constant pain. X-rays revealed that a disc in my lower back was not properly formed. The jumping incident instigated the defect and the ensuing pain that ignored my back but made my right leg ache.

Our family doctor recommended that I give up basketball. He stated that I'd be in constant pain and could possibly injure my back further. He thought paralysis was unlikely, but warned that it was a slight risk. My mother, though, couldn't bring herself to forbid me to play. She said that even though she didn't want me to play, she knew that I was old enough to make my own decisions. She also pointed out that one way or another, I was the one who would have to live with the consequences. Even then, I couldn't quite picture my life without basketball. I decided to play.

Shooting all of those baskets in my driveway had paid off. Coach had moved up to Varsity and asked me to move up, too. Usually, Varsity is for juniors and seniors so, as a sophomore, I felt honored. I readily agreed and was elated that I had persisted in playing this game.

As I lay on the floor, however, I wondered if I had made the right decision. After what seemed like a long time, I knew I had to try to stand. I closed my eyes and pushed myself up. My legs worked, in fact, everything worked but I was very shaken and felt extremely weak. Coach helped me to the bench where I watched the rest of the game.

Back on the bus, I felt like the last thing I cared about was slipping away. What would I do if I couldn't play basketball? Most days, it was the only reason I did my schoolwork. I didn't care about my grades anymore but I knew I had to pass if I wanted to play on the team. What would be my motivation for even getting up in the morning if I didn't have basketball? But, what if I did get injured again and the outcome wasn't so great? I thought I had paid the ultimate price tonight. I'm not even 16 and I really don't want to spend the rest of my life paralyzed.

Now standing next to me, Coach asked, "Are you okay?"

"I think so," I said. And, then, "I don't know."

Coach paused before responding. He stood there and I knew he didn't know what to say. It didn't matter, though, because I didn't know what I wanted to hear.

"You should come in and eat," he advised.

After school the next day, I stopped by the gym to inform Coach that I wouldn't be attending practice. He looked relieved. I think he had worried that I was there to quit the team. But, that decision hadn't been made yet.

I cleaned my assigned rooms in record time and went home. It was Friday and I was thankful to have the weekend to decide whether or not I should continue to play basketball. The house was quiet but I went to my room to be alone anyway. Dana had moved into David's old room after Donna had graduated and moved out. I liked having my own space. I had spent a lot of time arranging the top of the dresser I no longer had to share and now found comfort in the special items. I had my record player and a few trophies displayed.

My most prized item, however, was a little plastic Milwaukee Brewers baseball hat. I had bought it at a Brewers game that Dana and I had gone to the summer before David had died. It was a trip for "underprivileged" kids from throughout the Upper Peninsula. I imagine the idea was to show the small town kids the big city. Having been to Chicago to visit Mom's family a number of times, I wasn't impressed. But I did like staying in the hotel and going to the baseball game. I hadn't done either one of those things before.

The elevator at the hotel proved to be quite popular. We crammed in as many twelve and thirteen year olds as we could, and pushed the panel buttons. All the numbers were lit, as we rode from floor to floor. After many adult guests complained about the slow and crowded elevators, we were banned from that pastime for the remainder of our stay.

Next, we ran up and down the halls, visiting one another's rooms. We were stopped from that activity, as well, so we all ran down the stairs to the pool. We happily splashed, laughed, and swam until it was time to go to bed.

The next day, we went to the ball game. The crowds, noises and smells were slightly overwhelming. We had all been given a few dollars to spend on a souvenir so I pushed my way to the cashier and bought the small plastic hat.

It wasn't so much the hat that was special, but its contents. Inside the hat, I stored marbles that had belonged to David. I poured the marbles on my bed and sat next to them. Because of my back, I slept on a very firm mattress that barely moved whenever I did. It provided a nice, flat surface. I studied each individual marble and especially liked the cat-eyes. They were so different than the others and I appreciated their uniqueness. After looking at the marbles for a while, I scooped them back into their container and returned them to the top of my dresser.

Later that night, I drew the covers back and crawled into bed. I turned off my bedside lamp and started my prayers.

It was really more of a chant. "Dear Lord," I began, "please take care of David." I repeated it a few times, in case He was taking another break and didn't hear me the first time. I prayed this same prayer every night. Tonight, though, I couldn't stop and I found myself begging the Lord to send me a sign that my brother was okay. Any sign will do, I bargained. Begging the Lord turned into begging David. I sobbed into my pillow so neither Mom nor Dana would hear me and alternated between begging God and pleading with David to give me a sign, any sign, to indicate that he was okay. That's all I wanted to know, I pleaded. "Just send me a sign that you are okay."

A marble dropped off my bed and rolled across the tile

floor. The tears stopped instantly as I froze in my bed. Did I just imagine that? This definitely fell under the "Be careful what you wish for" category because I was now too frightened to move.

"David, was that really you? Are you really okay?" I had asked for a sign and now, apparently, I had gotten one. I couldn't believe I was asking for verification.

I must have left a marble on the bed, I told myself.

But how could I have pulled back the covers, gotten into bed, arranged my pillow, and gotten comfortable without that marble falling off? I shot back.

It could happen, I said.

Not in this twin bed that's as hard as a rock, it couldn't, I replied.

I decided to stop debating myself. I was getting nowhere. Maybe it was David, or God, and maybe it wasn't. Maybe he or He was sending me a sign or maybe it was just a coincidence. I chose to believe that it was David and God. Even though I desperately missed him and wanted him back more than ever, I was relieved to know that he was okay.

As I left for school Monday morning, I was carrying my gym bag. I had pushed the subject of basketball aside all weekend and put off making any decision. I think I knew I would return. I couldn't quit. I didn't care about anything else. What would I do without it? I didn't want to find out.

11

Second Winter

I've learned that saying, "I hate Christmas," is a conversation ender. Basketball season is over and I'm taking Driver's Education. A few nights after school, we practice driving with the teacher. At the end of our required time tonight, the conversation turned to the upcoming holiday. The driver, a guy in my class, stated that he loves Christmas as he pulled into my driveway to drop me off. He described how special the season is because of the lights, food, and the chance to spend time with family.

I saw our lighted tree glowing through the picture window. We didn't shop for a tree this year. Instead, Louis stopped by the house one evening and unloaded the evergreen from his truck. I was thankful that we didn't have to keep up the façade of happily choosing a tree. We hung the lights and the ornaments, baked the cookies, and made plans for Christmas day. But, looking at the house from the driveway, I was struck with how dark and cold our home seemed. It may have looked like any other house in town, but I knew it wasn't.

It was difficult to listen to him talk about how I knew Christmas should be. It had been like that once for me, too. Oh, how I loved all of it. Going to church and being part of the Christmas play, baking cookies for the neighbors, and making or buying gifts for our family. My siblings and I would draw names so we'd only have to give one gift instead of three. I always hoped to choose

David's name. I knew Donna and Dana had a close connection and I believed that David and I shared one, too. I had especially loved the Christmas music. Listening to "Silent Night" made the world seem so peaceful and full of hope.

There was even a time when I would feign sleep on Christmas Eve, and then creep out of bed when I was certain every one else had dozed off. I'd plug in the tree lights and gaze quietly at the softly shining colors and then longingly at the gifts under the tree. I loved gently handling the brightly wrapped boxes and trying to guess what was inside.

One year, I dared to carefully unwrap a present that was labeled for all of us. I quietly played with the slide projector and was awed when I saw Cinderella's castle reflected on the living room wall. After coaxing the gift back into its paper, I tiptoed back to bed with a huge smile on my face. I was just as excited to see it again the next morning.

I interrupted my classmate's offerings with, "I hate Christmas." No explanation, just the statement. The conversation ceased and we all sat there for a short time.

"Well, I guess I'll see you tomorrow," I said and got out of the car.

I'm finally a licensed driver. Freedom. Louis completely surprised me by giving me a car for my sixteenth birthday. After the divorce, he stayed away for some time, but then slowly worked his way back into our lives. First, it was by offering to buy school clothes in the fall. He'd agree to pay for them if we met him at the mall and let him spend time with us. My mother had to come, too. She had tried to convince him that his sister should take us to meet him, but he wouldn't agree to it. She accepted this arrangement because she felt she had no choice. She couldn't afford to buy us all the new school clothes we needed, but he could. And now, apparently, he had bought me a car.

Louis knew that Donna and Mom had had some of their worst fights over the one car and he didn't want Mom to go through that again. But, Mom and I never fought like that anyway. When they fought, there was a lot of yelling and door slamming. I didn't fight with Mom. Instead, I would ignore her. I could go for days without talking to her until she forced me to talk things over with her. But, just in case, Louis wanted to avoid any problems.

Mom drove me to Aunt's house, where the car was parked. Since it was February, it was already dark outside. On the way, she told me that we were going to see my new car. She said that Louis had been looking for a used vehicle for months and had finally found one in his price range. She told me that the car was a good deal and it ran well.

"He has agreed to pay for the insurance as long as you don't get any tickets. If you do, he'll drop you from his policy," she explained. "You have to pay for the gas and all of the maintenance."

We pulled into the driveway, and I caught sight of the two-door Ford Torino Cobra with incredible looking sport slats on the rear window. Wide, black, racing stripes ran down the hood of the car. I caught my breath and heard an unrecognizable noise escape from my mouth.

Mom laughingly stated, "That's the first time I've ever heard you squeal."

I jumped out of the passenger's seat and ran to Louis, who was dangling a set of car keys in my direction. As Mom's headlights shone on the car, I circled it before climbing into the driver's seat. Even in the dim light, I could see that my car was green.

12

Third Spring

It's May again. Two years since David's death. Our town is preparing for the annual Memorial Day Festival and parade. Every year the school's gym is converted to a small carnival where the young children can play games, try to win at the Cake Walk, and anxiously hope to be the one shouting, "Bingo!"

For the parade, the men and women who have served in the armed forces will don their old military uniforms and lead the floats through town. Many of my friends' fathers have served and they always seem to walk a little taller on this one day, wearing that uniform. Before the parade, I know, they've ridden a school bus to the local cemeteries to honor the military dead. We all know it's for the veterans, but we also honor our dead, too.

Days before, it is common to see the townspeople at their loved ones' graves, tidying the area and planting fresh flowers. We didn't do it right after David died. Only a few weeks had gone by and it was too difficult to view the fresh dirt that covered his grave. It was like looking at an open wound. Besides, Mom was still avoiding the cemetery. I had heard them fire the shots and play taps at the cemetery near our house and that was enough for me.

I did go the following year, though. I found the experience painful and comforting all at the same time. I was glad the veterans hadn't been forgotten. When I looked around and saw the families dispersed at their loved ones grave sites, I knew the other dead were also not forgotten. Family even represented many of the ones who had died years ago. I wouldn't make it to David's grave this time, however. I had someplace I had to be.

This year, the parade planners decided to have a Memorial Day Queen float in the parade. The ninth, tenth, and eleventh grade classes each elected two representatives and then all students voted for the queen. I was pleasantly surprised when the crown was presented to me. I was excited about riding on the float with the other girls who had been elected to the court. Aunt made it more special when she stopped by our house to take numerous pictures. Everyone said that the blue dress I was wearing perfectly matched the color of my eyes.

13

Third Summer

I'm working at school again this summer. I'm grateful for the routine as it makes the days go by faster. When I'm not working or shooting baskets, I get lost in the writings of John Steinbeck. *Of Mice and Men. The Grapes of Wrath. The Red Pony. The Pearl. The Winter of our Discontent.* I've read them all. Strangely, I find solace in the lonely struggles of many of the characters. The angst envelops me and assures me I'm not the only one to feel so disconnected and alone.

When will this pain stop? I spend hours alone in the woods, thankful for the relief it always provides. I lose all thought as I quietly follow the deer path that sneaks through the land my stepfather owns. Once, I even came upon a doe and her fawn sleeping in a field. The doe saw me, but did not run off. I was no threat to her. Another time, I was excited to see a buck cross the path less than thirty yards away. I didn't scare him either. I imagine all of the animals in the forest as my friends. I like the rocks and trees, too, and try not to play favorites.

I wander through my friends, the trees, but never get lost. I find my way to a favorite clearing, spread out a wool blanket, and lie down with my book. When I feel sleepy, I roll onto my back and close my eyes. I listen to the nearby bees buzzing from wildflower to wildflower, the grasshoppers jumping inches from my head, and the gentle breeze rustling the leaves.

"I could stay here forever," I often sigh and truly

believe it. If there is a God, this is where I would find him. Here, in the woods, I feel a connection to something. The planet? Mother Nature? Or is it God?

Renewed, I find my way back to my car. I then drive along the dirt road that cuts through the property. I love the way I leave the light behind as I am covered by the trees canopy. I turn the radio off, roll down the window and strain to hear the sounds of nature over the noise of the car's engine. Soon, I emerge from the canopy and am warmed by the sun's glow once again.

On my way home, I drive right by the cemetery, so I stop for a little visit with my brother. God must have a sense of humor because as I pull into the gravel path that leads to David's plot, Billy Joel's "Only the Good Die Young" often begins to play on the radio.

"Ain't that the truth," I reply.

14

We had to write an essay for English class. The topic was of our choosing, so I chose friendship. It only had to be a few paragraphs long. I didn't expect to read it aloud in class. Mr. Mortenson hadn't said anything about that when he had given us the assignment.

When he called on me to stand and read, I considered saying, "No." I didn't want to read this in front of everyone. It was too personal. Yet, I was more afraid of saying no to my teacher than I was of sharing such personal emotions with my classmates. So, I stood and pretended to clear my throat. I was really trying to reach deep inside for the strength to get through this without losing it.

"I used to think friendship was a word that could be tossed around lightly," I began. "Friends were there to ride bikes with after school or to just hang out with during the long summer days. I thought that if we liked the same activities, TV shows, or songs on the radio, we could be friends."

"But, then something happened," I stopped for a moment because I sensed the stillness that ensued. My classmates were no longer shifting in their chairs, or doodling on their notebooks. They were waiting for me to continue.

"But, then something happened," I repeated, "and I knew that friendship was much deeper than that.

Friendship is having the courage to call someone and listen to her cry, even when you don't know what to say." I wanted to look at Mary, the only one who had called me immediately after David died. I couldn't though. My face was already hot as it burned with embarrassment. I just had to finish this and sit down.

I went on to explain how friendship was about doing things together, yes, but it was also about being present when someone was in pain. It was about listening when someone wanted to talk but it was also about being silent when someone didn't want to talk. It was about taking someone by the hand and saying, "Lean on me, and together we'll get through this."

When I had written the essay, I had thought of Mary's call, but mostly, about my friend Tammy. Even though I had pushed her away the day David had died, she didn't stay away. Following David's death, we had spent a lot of time together. When it was so quiet at home, I could always count on Tammy to liven things up. She was a year ahead of me in school, but that never mattered. The only times I ever got into trouble during that time, I was with her. She was just what I needed. Last year, however, she had started dating someone and didn't have as much time for me. It was okay. We still played on the same basketball team and usually sat near one another on the long bus rides to away games. Even though we didn't spend as much time together now, I knew that I had learned how friendships should be from her example.

"So," I concluded, "when you are in a friendship, value it. It is more important than you might ever realize." I finished and quickly sat down. I stared at the essay I had returned to the top of my desk. Mr. Mortenson didn't say anything. Nothing. Was he thinking that he should reach out to me somehow? After all this time, it was clear that I was still thinking about David. He was silent, but I could feel the compassion in the room, from him and my classmates.

Finally, he said, "Next," and we mercifully moved on.

15

Third Winter

I was elected to Homecoming Court this year. The junior and senior classes vote for two boys and two girls to represent each class. Then the whole high school votes for the king and the queen. Usually, the ones crowned are from the senior class.

I was surprised to be selected. I've always gotten along well with the boys in my class, but most of my friends are either a year ahead or a year behind me. Only one other girl in our class participates in sports and she and I have never really seen eye to eye. No reason, really, just one of those things. The other girls aren't interested in basketball, so I don't think we have much in common.

We all used to be friends, however, in grade school. I remembered all of the sleepovers when we were younger and the hours we spent talking about our families, our teachers and the boys in our class. Many of us had learned basic sign language from the encyclopedia so we could communicate in class when the teacher's back was turned. What we had to say was too important to wait until recess and too risky to put down on a note that could be intercepted. So, we'd pay attention until the teacher looked away and then our fingers would start flying.

When a few of the boys caught on to what we were doing, they, too, learned the language. We stopped signing soon afterwards. As we approached middle school, and then high school, we developed different interests.

My best friend, Kelly, is a year younger. We have always known each other because she's in Dana's grade. Dana, another friend named Nikki, and Kelly used to meet at our house before David died to practice their cheering before the middle school games. I hated it. I'd roll my eyes at Mom as I made a big fuss about leaving the living room. She'd always laugh while Dana and her friends continued to clap and bounce around. I think they cheered louder after I had left the room, trying to reach me through the closed door of my bedroom.

Kelly and Dana had grown apart, but we had struck up a conversation during study hall one day. At first, I thought she was talking to me because I was about to get my driver's license and she still had another year to wait. It didn't matter. After all, Tammy was spending more and more time with her boyfriend so I needed a new friend. Kelly still cheered for the boys' games, but she also played basketball, so I didn't hold the cheering against her.

We became fast friends and spend many hours riding around the area on Friday and Saturday nights. We have a standing arrangement that if we aren't asked out on a date by Wednesday, we will hang out together on the weekend. Neither one of us have ever broken our agreement. I'm not asked out much, so it's pretty easy to honor that promise.

We often wonder about our friends who do get asked out a lot and spend all of their free time with their boyfriends. Those relationships always seem so fluid. One week they are dating, the next they aren't. There are no guarantees. Kelly and I, though, are friends. By the very nature of the word, we are supposed to be loyal to one another. We have each other's backs. We often speak about how we'll still be calling each other when we are old women.

As we spend many nights cruising through Carney and the neighboring town of Nadeau, we discuss the present and, sometimes, the future. Where will we go? What will we do? Who will we be?

Our future seems to lie before us like a never-ending highway. We plan our plans and dream our dreams but putting them into action is just beyond our capabilities. We aren't prepared to go that far yet. Reminiscent of the turn around point on Highway 41, we can only go so far before we have to stop, spin around, and return home. The weekends spent with one another are slowly turning into years as we maneuver our way through high school.

16

Fourth Spring

"Have you heard the bad news?" Tom asked as I slid into the seat next to him during homeroom.

After I shook my head, he continued. "K's mother and six siblings died in a fire during the night. I drove past their house this morning before school. It's completely destroyed."

K had been our classmate until she quit school last year. She and a few others in our class dropped out soon after turning sixteen. K and I had never been close, but our school was small and we only had one class for each grade level. I had gone to school with her since kindergarten. The rest of us were now in eleventh grade.

Within a few days, the school held a memorial service. Most of the children had attended school so many classes were affected by this loss. For my brother's class, it was the second time in three years that they had lost a classmate and friend.

We filed into the gym by grade level and found our place in the bleachers. The younger children were sitting with crossed legs on the floor. It was very quiet and only the sounds of us stepping onto the bleachers could be heard. I noticed the chairs, podium and microphone that were placed in the middle of the gym floor. I saw Pastor B and the priest from the Catholic Church already seated up front. I figured the principal and superintendent would also sit up there. But who would occupy the other two chairs? As if in reply, I saw K and her father being led to the seats.

Oh, no, I thought. *I can't believe they are making her sit up there.* I felt ashamed. She was grieving and, yet, she had to be on display for all of us. It seemed so cruel. Slumped in the chair with her arms crossed, her body language clearly indicated that she did not want to be there. Out of respect, I tried not to stare but I found my eyes returning to her as I tuned out what all of the adults were saying to try to make sense of this tragedy.

I had lost one sibling. She had lost all six of hers, along with her mother. I knew her father had a drinking problem and wasn't even living with the family when they all died. K hadn't been living at home, either. She was completely on her own. Was she even seventeen yet?

After the service, I wanted to talk to her. But what would I say? I knew how it felt to lose a sibling, but I didn't know how she felt losing all six of hers and her mother. She looked so angry with her father, the adults trying to offer comfort, and all of us trying not to stare at her. In fact, she looked angry at the entire world. I had no idea what to say to her and I doubted she'd let me hold her hand.

17

Fourth Summer

Wait. Wait. Wait. I feel like all I'm doing is waiting. Waiting to graduate, waiting to leave home, waiting to go to college. It's only the summer before my senior year, so it's going to be a long wait.

I try not to be at home as much as possible. Ever since David died, we've all just lived together. I think our family died on that day in May. We have survived, but that's all we've done. We haven't grown any closer; in fact, we are all distant from one another. Donna has joined the Army and only occasionally calls home. Dana is just a year younger than I, but we have different friends and seldom do things together. We are both spending the summer working for Aunt since the summer jobs at school went to other students. (I still have my job after school, though, since it's considered a different program.) The only time we spend together during the day is the five-minute car ride there and back. Once there, she helps Aunt in the office, while I help Louis outside and in the garage. So far this summer, I've plowed a spot for a garden, shoveled out the chicken coop and the pigsty, and did odd chores in the truck garage. I'm not too sure what Dana does. Louis gets mad at Aunt, his sister, and tells her to send Dana outside to work. She never listens to him. I don't care. I prefer to be outside, anyway. Plus, Louis doesn't talk a whole lot, and I like the quiet.

At home, Mom does talk but I'm not interested in what

she has to say. Since we never talk about the past, I can only think about the future. She seems more interested in the present, so I tune her out.

Sometimes, I look at Mom and wonder, *Is this the same person from all those years ago? I wonder if she is the same woman who would come to my bedside when I wasn't feeling well as a young girl. Were those her hands that always felt so cool and gentle on my forehead? Was she the one I would sit with in the bathroom and have interesting conversations?*

It might sound strange, but I loved sitting in there when she was soaking in the bathtub. She never seemed to mind when I would slip in and sit on the closed toilet seat. She'd put her book aside and we'd have a pleasant little chat. Why did we stop talking?

Was it her who used to take us on picnics to the nature park in a nearby town? We couldn't afford to eat out, but we would stop and buy sub sandwiches at the deli in the discount store. We'd divide them up and share them on the blanket that was stored in the car's trunk. Was she the same person who would drive us to the swimming hole and spend the entire afternoon lazily lying in the sun, reading a book while we splashed and swam the day away? She'd pack a lunch for us and would wait until we proclaimed that we were dying from hunger.

"Get the cooler," she'd say, without even looking up from her book.

I miss those days and that feeling of us being a family. I miss feeling connected to something bigger than myself.

18

I woke up late and had to run all the way to school so I wouldn't be marked tardy. When I got to English class, I realized I had left my textbook at home. It had my homework in it. We had a pop quiz in history and I was sure I flunked it because I hadn't read the assigned chapters.

It would have been—should have been—David's thirteenth birthday. He would have been an official teenager. As I had walked to basketball practice, I wondered if the day could get any worse.

I soon found out that the answer was, yes, it could. After running our required laps, I started towards the drinking fountain for some water. The line was long at the one in the gym, so I pushed through the double doors and headed to the fountain in the hallway. Coach stopped me before I could get to it.

"I'm going to start Shirley for our next game," he told me. "She's been working really hard and I think she deserves a chance in the starting lineup. It's what's best for the team."

He paused, and then said, "She'll be starting in your position."

I was stunned. I wanted to say, "No, don't do this, especially not today. I've always started. I can try harder. Just give me another chance."

But, I didn't say anything except, "Ok." Fortunately, I

was right in front of the girls' bathroom, and I quickly ducked in there. I was relieved he couldn't follow me because I didn't want him to see me cry. I slid to the floor, pulled my knees to my chest, and put my head down.

As I was crying, I began to question myself. Why was I crying? Why was I *really* crying? Was it for basketball and losing my starting spot? I was disappointed and even slightly embarrassed. I had always started. What would the others say? But was I really crying because of that? Or was I crying for David? As soon as I thought it, I knew it was true. I had been holding it in through the long, frustrating day.

I still missed him so much. Would that ever stop? It'd been three and half years and I still thought about him all of the time. Even though I never heard anyone talk about him, even at home, he was always in my thoughts. Thankfully, he had returned to my dreams, too. He was happy in my dreams. It still hurt to think about losing him, but I had grown accustomed to the pain. I knew it hadn't gone away; I had just gotten used to it. Now, I could remember some of the fun times we shared and not feel so sad. But the emptiness was always there.

Basketball had sustained me these past four seasons. I don't think I could have survived without it. It gave me a reason to get up in the morning, a reason to go to school, a reason to complete my assignments. I never thought about life after high school or the need to get good grades so that I could attend college. I only thought about passing my classes so that I could play basketball. I had needed basketball.

But maybe that wasn't so true anymore. I wasn't going

to quit, of course, but maybe I could stand on my own now. It was my last season, anyway. In a way, I had felt like I had peaked. I was in constant pain from my back and had already scheduled a surgery for after the season. Everyone else on the team continued to improve while I seemed to be standing still. I was still working hard but it just wasn't enough.

I loved basketball because we won or lost as a team. It was bigger than just one person; bigger than just me. I was a part of something that needed and depended on me to do my best. All those years spent practicing, the summer basketball camps I had attended, and the hours lost in thought about how I could improve weren't just for me. Of course, I wanted to be a good individual player; we all did. In the end, though, it was the team that benefited. I still cared about the team and I did want what was best for it. Shirley was working hard and she deserved to start. I stood, splashed cold water in my face, dried my eyes and returned to the gym.

A few games later, I was starting again. A few games after that, Shirley started. Following a practice one afternoon, Shirley and I found ourselves alone in the locker room.

"I'm sorry, Diane," she said. "I never tried to take your starting position."

I stopped packing my gym bag and turned to speak to her.

"Shirley, I've never had hard feelings toward you. If anything, I'm mad at Coach. I wish he'd make up his mind already. But you work hard at practice and in the games and so do I."

"That's true," she said. "Besides, I was thinking about

how there are five starting positions, not just one. Maybe we'll both start during one of the games."

I looked at her mischievous grin and laughed.

"That's right," I agreed. "There are five starting positions."

19

Fourth Winter

Dana, Nikki, Kelly and I were all crowded into our small bathroom. We jockeyed for position in front of the two mirrors as we prepared for Homecoming. Nikki and I had both been selected for the Homecoming Court and Dana and Kelly were helping us get ready. The queen would be crowned before the boys' varsity basketball game.

"Oh, Dia," Kelly exclaimed, "I forgot to bring that necklace you wanted to borrow. I need to run home to get it."

Then it was Nikki's turn. "Oh, no! I forgot my jewelry, too."

Kelly left in her car and Dana took mine to drive Nikki home.

"Hurry back," I yelled after them as they rushed out the door. I was alone. Even though the stereo still blasted away in the living room, I felt a quiet fall over the house. Then I heard it. The first few notes, so hauntingly familiar, began to play.

Not now, I immediately thought. I didn't want to hear that song, David's song, right now.

"Too late," I whispered and waited for the sadness to wash over me. Instead, I was filled with a peaceful feeling that I had never experienced prior to that moment. I placed the curling iron on the counter and stared at myself in the mirror. I looked the same on the outside. On the inside, though, I knew I had changed. I was going to be all right. *I was going to be all right.* I had survived the unimaginable. Was I stronger? Maybe. I didn't know for sure. But I hadn't turned to drugs or alcohol or even tried to end it all. I was still here and I was still standing. Somehow, I had endured. I remembered being so angry when Mom had David's dog shot. I believed TJ had been the last living thing connected to my brother. Now, however, I realized that even though David was physically gone, a part of him would always be with me. For so long, I had thought that a part of me had died with David and was buried with him in that cemetery. That still felt true, but it also felt true that he still lived in me. Instead of TJ, I was a living thing connected to David. In fact, all of us who loved David were still connected to him. His memory and, maybe, even his spirit continued to live through us. Indeed, at that moment, I had a strong sense that he was there wishing me good-luck.

When the crown was placed on my head later that night, I knew David was watching.

"Thank you, little brother," I offered up to him.

David was almost taken from us once before his actual death. When he was nearly two years old, he suffered from allergies and had to take the prescribed medicine twice a day. Louis, who was still living with us at the time, would give David the morning dose, feed him breakfast, and put him back to bed before leaving for work. This time, however, the cap to the bottle wasn't placed back on tightly. As Louis was preparing to leave for work, Mom arose to check on David. She noticed that more than expected was missing from the medicine bottle. She frantically called for Louis and woke his mother who was also residing with us at that time. Grandma called the nearest emergency room while Mom and Louis gathered David from his bed and carried him to the kitchen. It would be a thirty-minute car ride and they were advised by the ER staff not to take it.

"You must keep him awake. If he falls asleep, he could possibly die," they were warned.

They were told to take him outside and make him walk. If he were still alive in a few hours, he would be okay. So, they quickly got themselves and my brother dressed and went outside.

Up and down the road they went, begging David not to fall asleep. They sang to him, told him stories and bribed him to stay awake.

"We'll take you to the store later and let you pick out something," they bargained.

As our neighbors prepared for the day, they noticed Mom, Louis and David outside. Soon, all five families who lived nearby were out there taking turns. By this time, David could not stand unsupported, so he was flanked on either side by a neighbor. As their own children peacefully eased into a new day, they helped fight for my brother's life as they practically dragged him up and down the road. One woman went into her house and returned with a thermos of coffee and cups for all. As David cried from exhaustion, they kept walking. As the hours slowly ticked by, they kept walking. As the sun finally began to warm the blacktop, they kept walking. But now it was with lighter hearts because their prayers had been answered. David was still alive.

In my heart, I knew that if we had lost him then, I

wouldn't have grieved so deeply. I would've only been six years old. I would've missed him, sure, but not like I do now.

So, I wondered. If I had to lose him anyway, would I have rather had him die when he was two, instead of nine? I wouldn't have been so close to him so I wouldn't have suffered nearly as much. The thought was easily entertained but horrifying, too. If I could rip those years from my mind, would I? Most of the pain of losing him would be gone. In its place would be a vague memory of a baby brother. Would I choose that?

I knew I wouldn't. If I could erase the pain, the cost would be too high. I loved having him in my life. I loved having him in our family. I loved being a "little mother" to him and checking his homework and tucking him in at night. I always told him I loved him, but he told me that he loved me, too. I loved teaching him how to ride a bike, shoot a basketball, and throw a football. I loved teasing him about his messed up hair that always seemed to hang in his eyes. I loved watching him eat cold ravioli from a can, even though I found it disgusting. I loved how he could eat ketchup between two pieces of bread when he was too lazy to make a proper sandwich. I'd laugh and express my doubts when he claimed to like it. I loved having him in my life because I loved him. I wouldn't have given that up for anything.

20

Fifth Spring

The snow has melted and I can easily walk in the woods again. I can't drive along the path, though, because of the mud. No matter. I just want to walk.

A few more months of school and a summer and I'll be on my way to college. I can hardly wait. I want to leave all of this behind and start over.

As always, while walking through the woods, I felt a pull. The past few months have found me thinking about God. Was I being called back to Him? When I get settled at college, I know I will find a church. I'm looking forward to it.

I have always wanted to be a part of a strong, traditional family. Especially after David's death, I've looked at my friends' families with envy. Would I ever have that? Once, a few years ago, Mom asked us what we wanted when we grew up. Donna wanted a good paying job and a successful career. Dana wanted to travel and see the different cities of the world. Those plans sounded great to me, too, but what I really wanted was a loving husband, a couple of children, and a nice home. Mom took it all in, turned to me and stated that mine would be the hardest to get.

Maybe I wouldn't get it, I feared, but I knew how I could become part of a traditional "family." Most of my friends were Catholic and through the years I had heard them talking about the classes they attended and all of the different rituals they followed throughout the year. They had to attend weekly confessions, memorize assigned prayers, give up something important during the Lenten season, honor the Holy days, and, of course, all the other holidays that all Christians shared. A few times, I had gone to Mass with Kelly. Each time, except for the readings and the homily, the service was the same. They knelt at the same time; they stood at the same time. Every Sunday, it was the same. It didn't get any more traditional than that.

Before I left for college, though, I believed I should attend a service in our former church. I felt liked I owed the church that much.

It was a beautiful day, so I decided to walk. I remembered all those times I walked to church as a child. When I neared the front doors, I hesitated. I was nervous. Would everyone be whispering and pointing, "Look who's here?" I slid through the door and headed straight to the bathroom. I hid in a stall and had a little chat with God.

Ok, I'm here. Now what?

I waited. Nothing.

This isn't enough, is it? I suppose you want me to go upstairs.

Still nothing.

Fine, I'll go. But, please, stay with me.

I ascended the stairs. I hadn't been in the church since Jonathan's funeral but it hadn't changed, although Pastor B was no longer there. Over the stairs leading to the basement, I had seen the familiar words to "How Great Thou Art." As far as I knew, those words had always been there. I wondered if they still ended the service with that hymn.

I walked through the entry and was handed a bulletin. I didn't notice anyone pointing but I caught a few stares. It was okay; I was surprised to see myself there, too.

I sat down and pretended to read the printed announcements in the bulletin. A girl I knew from school sat ahead of me with her family.

She turned around and asked, "Would you like to sit with us?"

Grateful for her kindness, I accepted.

The service was nice and I was so pleased when I heard the beginning notes to "How Great Thou Art," but I knew I wouldn't be back. I realized I had come to say good-bye. Good-bye to this type of religion that I really didn't know too well. Good-bye to this congregation that didn't help my mother when she so desperately needed it. Good-bye to this congregation that did help when David died. Good-bye to this church.

I didn't know where I would be led in my search for belonging. Would I become a Catholic, or a Baptist, or a Lutheran, or a Methodist? I didn't know.

I did know that there was nothing "wrong" with this church or its congregation. But, sometimes, it's just easi-er to call it a scratch and start all over elsewhere.

It's May again. This month marks the fourth anniversary of David's death. It's strange how it feels like it has been such a long time since I've seen him and, yet, it also feels like he just died last week.

I still miss him. I think I always will.

The university I will be attending in the fall offered an early orientation program for the in-coming students from the Upper Peninsula. The principal offered me a full tank of gas if I would drive three others and myself to the orientation. I readily accepted the deal: A free tank of gas, a day away from school, and the chance to laugh and joke with three guys from my class. How could I refuse?

We met at the school and got an early start. We laughed and reminisced during the two-hour drive. Once there, we went to our individual programs and then met again for the return trip.

On the way home, we all excitedly shared the details of our day apart. We had seen the dorms where we would live. None of us wanted to live in a coed dorm and I was pleased when I realized that the all-girls dorm and the all-boys dorm were connected and we'd be sharing many planned activities.

We talked about the few people we knew attending the university and the advice they had given us. We all wished the rest of the school year and summer would fly right by so we could get on with our lives.

After dropping the guys off at school, I drove towards home. As I turned onto the road that led to my house, I saw a flash of color. I quickly pulled off the road and got out of my car. I looked at the hillside that flanked the town's cemetery and caught my breath.

"You're back!" I said aloud. The lilacs were in bloom. The beautiful, heavenly scented, purple lilacs were back.

The last day of high school finally arrived. The exams were done. None of us even knew why we were still attending school because we mostly just played games or talked. Even the class list of "Who's Who" had been decided. The "Most Likely to Succeed," the "Most Athletic," and the "Most Humorous" had all been named.

The "Most Likely to Succeed" always confused me. How do you measure success? Is it the one who makes the most money? But what if he or she hates the job and doesn't have time for anything else? Is that still a success? What about the guys in my class who wanted nothing more than to be farmers like their fathers? If they made that happen for themselves, wouldn't they be successful, too?

I looked around the room at these people. I had known most of them since kindergarten but I wondered: *Did I really know them?* They had no idea what I went through after losing David. I recalled the many conversations we had shared at various activities. We always talked, but never really *talked*. What if, just once, I had said, "I still miss David so much?" What if, instead of waiting for others to bring up his name, I spoke of him first? I know they would have listened, just as I would have listened to them if they had confided in me.

I thought back to that awful day in the gym, when K was obviously grieving the death of her family. I didn't know what to say, so I said nothing. I wished I'd at least looked her in the eye and admitted, "I don't know what to say."

But I was afraid. I was afraid of how she'd react. I realized that for most people it's easier to say nothing; not out of a lack of compassion, but out of fear. It wasn't not caring or forgetting about the death, it's being afraid of saying the wrong thing. It's also being afraid to reach out for someone's hand and just hold it.

I suddenly recognized that I could have extended my hand and reached for comfort. These classmates, my teachers, and my own family would've helped. When I was drowning in my grief, they would've thrown me the life preserver. If I had signaled for help, I wouldn't have had to struggle to shore by myself.

I looked at my classmates again. What had they gone through to get to this point? Did some of them have their own private pain to endure? Perhaps we had more in common than I once thought. Maybe more than a few of us had already earned the "Successful" title.

I thought of our class motto. *The journey of a thousand miles begins with a single step.* What journeys would we be sharing at our ten-year or twenty-year class reunions?

I recalled a little trip Mom, Dana, and I had taken the previous summer. It was a few days spent visiting some of the sights around the Upper Peninsula. While we cruised along Lake Superior's shoreline and viewed the Pictured Rocks, my mind wandered. *What else would I get to see?* I was awakening to the fact that there was a whole wide world out there, just waiting for me. I dreamed of seeing Paris, London, and Rome. I especially longed to see Pompeii.

I didn't know what journey I would be sharing with my classmates at some future reunion. But I did know that I was more than ready to take that first step.

The school bell rang loud and clear. A cheerful noise burst forth from our classroom as the door swung open and we seniors spilled into the hall. No need to stop by lockers for they were emptied days ago. As a group, we moved towards the parking lot. Even the ones who didn't normally drive to school had done so today, because they, too, wanted to participate in this grand tradition.

I anxiously waited for Dana and Kelly to find me and climb into my car. We rolled down the windows, turned up the radio and found our place in line. One by one, my classmates laid on their horns as they revved their engines and prepared to squeal out of the school's driveway, one last time.

Finally, it was my turn. I pressed my car's horn, turned the radio even louder, and yelled for joy. I spun out of the driveway, smiled at my passengers and headed towards the rainbow of colors I could just make out on the edge of town.

AFTERWORD

It's been many years since I lost my brother. I still think of him on a regular basis and even, occasionally, dream about him. He still lives within me.

While in college, I decided to extend my hand and ask for help. I sought therapy through the campus counseling offices. I was fortunate to be paired with a wise counselor who gently guided me through many painful discussions about the loss of David and what it did to my family. I will never be able to express the deep gratitude I have for the time spent with this counselor and the profound change it made in my life.

Also during my years spent at college, I did search for a religion. I converted to Catholicism and practiced it for nearly ten years. Upon marrying my husband, I agreed to worship in the Lutheran church. (ELCA) The religions are very similar and I am comfortable with it. I still feel closest to God, though, when I am in the woods and I'm certain that will always be true for me.

Between the counseling and the strengthening of my religious beliefs, I am finally at peace with David's death. Sometimes bad things happen and we never know why. Writing this book has also been very cathartic and I can finally let the sorrow go.

My coming to terms with the loss has deepened my relationship with my sisters and mother. My sisters and I only occasionally discuss David but I know he still lives on within them. Mom and I often discuss him. We reminisce about the things he said or did and find ourselves laughing or shaking our heads during these conversations. He still lives in her, too. She was very encouraging during the process of my writing this story. A story such as this seldom belongs to just one person. It is her story, too, and although parts of it were painful for her to read, she never discouraged my truth. I am grateful to her for that allowance. Her truth might be different than mine, but we are both okay with that. The anger I displayed towards her dissipated years ago. Today, we share a healthy, open relationship. (Thanks, Mom!)

Shortly after Dana graduated from high school, Mom moved to Florida. She still hates the cold and won't even consider traveling to Michigan during the winter months. Although she doesn't visit often, Mom remains appreciative of the people of Carney who tried the best they knew how to help her through that terrible loss. She has told me many times about an older woman she barely knew who would occasionally send cards that said, "I'm thinking about you." Those few, short words displayed deep meaning and kindness that Mom will never forget.

For the record, Mom recently told me that she had our dog, TJ, taken to the Humane Society and not to a farm. She told us the farm story because she believed we would imagine him happy with a new family. To a rural kid, though, having a dog taken to "a farm" meant certain death. Having grown up in the city, she didn't realize that. I left the mis-assumption in the story because it played a vital role in the anger I directed at my mother. Miscommunications—and/or the lack of communication—add layers of confusion to grief, and I feel that scene strongly illustrates that.

Mom wanted me to mention that my sisters and I each

got what we had stated we wanted all those years ago. Over time, all of our spoken desires seemed to meld as we borrowed each other's dreams and tried them on for size.

Donna lived in a foreign country for eight years and was able to see many different places. She currently has a very successful career with the U.S. government. She also has two fantastic children, three great stepchildren, and an adoring husband.

Dana has lived in two foreign countries and has traveled to many interesting places. She and her husband returned to Carney and are now busy raising their two wonderful children there. She teaches at the same high school we attended and, in fact, her classroom belonged to my English teacher, Mr. Mortenson, all those years ago.

I've also done some traveling. I've been fortunate to live in three foreign countries and have traveled to many incredible places, including Paris, London, Rome, and, even, Pompeii. I have been an elementary school teacher and a school librarian. Currently, I am a seventh grade English teacher. My greatest joy, however, is my family.

My loving husband, Brad, has always supported my every endeavor. To whatever I want to attempt or to wherever I want to visit, he has always said "Yes, you should do it," or "Yes, let's go there!"

Together, we have two beautiful, incredible children. I love Katie and Ben more than life itself. I thank God for these joyous gifts everyday. Their presence in my life has healed many pains and has given me numerous reasons to smile.

It should also be noted that Kelly and I are still friends. Even though we live many states apart, I think of her often and we try to touch base with one another on a regular basis.

Before closing, I would like to express my many thanks to Pastor B. I believe God has had a hand in our reconnecting after almost thirty years. Pastor B was enthusiastic and encouraging when I told him about this project. He very generously offered to help get this published. Thank you.

Printed in the United States
134633LV00001B/43/P

9 780982 146606